Outside

CHRIS MCCULLY

TWO RAVENS
PRESS

Published by Two Ravens Press Ltd.
Taigh nam Fitheach
26 Breanish, Uig
Isle of Lewis HS2 9HB
United Kingdom

www.tworavenspress.com

ISBN: 978-1-906120-57-3

British Library Cataloguing in Publication Data: a CIP record for this book can be obtained from the British Library.

Designed and typeset in Sabon by Two Ravens Press; cover design by Two Ravens Press.

Cover photograph by Jan Zoetekouw, agency Dreamstime.

Printed in Poland on Forest Stewardship Council-accredited paper.

About the Author

Chris McCully is a freelance writer and academic who retains strong interests in angling and in the natural world. He has published over twenty books including six collections of poems (*Selected Poems* will appear from Carcanet in 2011), a memoir on addiction (*Goodbye, Mr. Wonderful*) and several book-length works on angling. In 2007 he moved with his wife and Labrador to Groningen, in the north-east of the Netherlands – and wrote about what he found there.

For more information about the author, see
www.tworavenspress.com

Textual note

I have generally transliterated Dutch or German proper names into their English equivalents, thus *Waddenzee* becomes 'Wadden Sea' and *Nordrhein-Westfalen* becomes 'North Rhine-Westphalia'.

For all my islands

Preface

Books occasionally happen by accident. *Outside* is largely the result of such an accident, which began one October day in 2008 on an afternoon hurling with rain. For some reason I don't now remember I decided to go for a walk – I was probably fed up with sitting in the study and working – and on an impulse took a digital camera with me.

Part of my route, haphazardly chosen, lay across the butt-end of a canal called the Boterdiep in the heart of Uithuizen, a small town which lies two miles from this desk. At the nexus of town and canal there's a miniature harbour, which in October 2008 was two-thirds empty of boats. I paused – I always pause, in and around harbours – and watched a group of men fishing in the deep water of the harbour's heart, in the boats' turning circle. The rain was sluicing down. Every now and then, one of the rods would flick quickly, the line would tighten, and a small roach would be brought to hand, unhooked, and slipped into a keep-net. Then the tackle would be readied again, the float would be lowered, and the angling process would recommence. Occasionally, one of the local roach experts would roll a cigarette one-handed under the shelter of an over-large umbrella, without taking his eyes off the float for an instant.

They were silent, focused and intent. They looked like a row of angling Buddhas, but without the smile. Traffic on the road behind us hissed past through huge puddles. I took out the camera and, shielding the lens with my left hand, took some snapshots: boats, semi-abandoned harbour, rain, and a row of angling gods.

When I got home I uploaded the photographs. One shot, lightly edited, was promising. It became even more promising when I edited it further into slight fuzziness. When I subsequently edited the remaining fuzz into black and white, I was content: the shot, I thought, captured the austere mood, the grey and yellow light. While I was fiddling with uploads and edits I continued to think about how intent and expert those local fishers were, and about the slow ferocity of concentration they brought to their art.

At that point, in terms of the structure of what was to be this book, I had done no more than go for a walk, watch some fishermen and take an interesting photo.

A week later and I went back to the same place, this time with a fishing rod in my hand. It was still raining – showers, not a deluge – and there, sitting on the harbour dock, was the same row of roach experts. I walked round to the opposite bank of the canal and began to fish for pike. (Pike will almost invariably lie around the edge of these big shoals of roach.) After twenty minutes, I caught and returned a jack, a fish of around 6lb. It was the first pike I'd taken that autumn.

Clearly, these local roach experts – the row of Buddhas, the silent concentration – had impressed me, because I began to draft a small piece which described them. I still don't know why I did this, although I know the impulse to write in order to re-possess and understand a perceived reality is a lifelong habit, and suspect it's probably a bad one. (In other words, one of the reasons I write anything at all is in some sense to 'make it real'. Often enough, I'm afraid, if I don't or can't write about something then I feel it – whatever 'it' is – has slipped away without being caught, intellectually seized, inspected and understood. For me, therefore, writing is a tacit rage for understanding. It's also a compulsion, and like all compulsions, an egocentric, anti-democratic one.)

At that point, in terms of the structure of what was to be this book, I had done no more than go for a walk; watch some fishermen; take an interesting photo; catch a pike; and draft 1200 words of prose.

I finished the draft in mid-afternoon. At teatime I had an email from Rosie Ward-Allen, one of my kind and expert publishers. In the course of her email, Rosie asked whether I perhaps had 'anything new' which might be submitted to *Waterlog*, a great angling journal to which I'd occasionally been lucky enough to contribute. I replied that in fact I'd just drafted a small piece – I stressed it was only a draft – and wondered whether that might meet requirements. I attached the draft to my note. (I was smiling to myself. Like any journalist, I was quietly asking 'Will this do?') Rosie's reply came within half an hour. She not only accepted the piece, but wondered if I had – or might eventually have – any more like it.

At that point, in terms of the structure of what was to be this book, I had done no more than go for a walk; watch some fishermen; take an interesting photo; catch a pike; draft 1200 words of prose ... and had sold them.

I've confessed that writing is perhaps a bad habit. I wondered, sitting again in the study confronting the screen, whether I might use the habit to help explain the realities which surrounded me in this northerly and relatively remote part of the Netherlands, to which we'd moved from Amsterdam in 2007. I admit here, as I've admitted to Monika, that I'd completely underestimated the cultural, even the linguistic changes which the move would necessitate. In truth, living in this region – locals call it *het Hogeland*, literally (and often somewhat ironically) 'the high land' – felt to me like a kind of beneficent exile. I felt a long way from home ... but where, after all, was 'home'?

The feeling of being 'outside' – outside my former employment as a full-time academic, outside any mainstream of writing and publishing, outside the circle of former friends and acquaintances – was intensified when in autumn 2008, after a great deal of thought, I applied for a full-time university job in Groningen. I was told bluntly that I didn't 'fit in'. I suppose it was kindly meant, and I even suppose it was true, but I began to wonder where on earth I did 'fit in'. What was I actually *for*?

One response was to go for another walk. The walk led down the banks of the local canal, the Usquerdermaar. On the banks, which twist through a series of meanders, I found some opened freshwater mussel shells. They were beautiful, since their nacre caught the drifts of high cloud and darkened very slightly as the cloud passed over the sun. I took another photograph. What was I for? Where did I fit in? What were freshwater mussels for? Where did *they* fit in?

When I got home I drafted another piece, this one about freshwater mussels. A week later, I was fishing for coastal sea-trout on the island of Funen, in Denmark. I caught one fish which took the fly adjacent to a dense mass of bladderwrack. As I slipped the fish gently back I wondered why bladderwrack was called 'bladderwrack' – and also wondered what the bladders of bladderwrack were for. Subsequently I drafted a piece about the structures of seaweeds ... and sold both the mussels and the bladderwrack to *Waterlog*.

By accident, therefore, I was on my way. Before long I'd drafted seven or eight *Outside* pieces. Each was around 1000-1200 words, most were accompanied by a black and white image, and each explored some aspect of the realities which seemed to surround me in this resolutely Dutch exile. After a while I gave up asking what I was for: I was working, and writing; describing these realities was, after all, part of 'what I was for'. After that, I just got on with it, and seemed to draft one such *Outside* piece almost every week.

Many of these pieces involve angling. I make no apology

for that, since angling isn't merely the catching of fish on rod and line but comprises all those fragments of animal and plant distribution and behaviour which together make up the contexts out of which this pastime begins. Accordingly, I tried to describe those contexts, as they are found both here in het Hogeland and in other places (Ireland, Denmark) I fished during the period 2008-09. Mussels, terns, seaweed, garfish; the habits of those summer shadows, the common carp; hawthorns and butterflies; frogs and starlight... They all were part of the realities I was attempting to describe in order to feel more in place. Even in the more 'urban' of these pieces – the description of a visit to London, for instance – the water is never far away, since in London, rather as in life, I was walking near, through or over rivers.

Writing these pieces helped me explore some of the topographies and history of this ancient Dutch landscape, whose acres are among the longest-settled in Europe. Understanding those cultures, histories and natural histories, all with their own intricacies, defeats, creativities and charms, involved me in some intensive reading (often in Dutch, since original records are in many cases unavailable in English) and equally intensive *looking*. That outwardly directed curiosity was a useful corrective, I found, to the baleful self-absorption that sometimes comes with the idea of 'exile'. Some of these researches shed interesting light on my mother tongue: it's doubtful, for instance, whether I'd ever have examined the lovely etymology of the word *kingfisher* without having first queried why kingfishers were called *ijsvogels* (literally, 'ice-birds') in Dutch.

I ask myself, finally, what these pieces are all about. As I've claimed above, they were and are 'about' being outside, sometimes with a fishing rod to hand and sometimes without one. Beyond what they describe, however, the pieces also gave me the opportunity to work in a new way at what is an odd word limit: 1200 words is, after all, neither short enough to be a filler nor long enough to be a feature article. Nevertheless, the 1200-word length which many of these pieces seemed to want to be was, I hope, adequate for my purposes since its ambit discouraged waffle but nevertheless could encompass the development of multiple themes – themes which are often recapitulated, in different contexts, from piece to piece. Technically, therefore, writing at this length was interesting. It's only now, two years on, that I realise the process was akin to what seems to happen when I construct verse. The difference is that verse often seems to grow from the nucleus of a rhythmically driven phrase whose meanings need to be in some sense 'sung'; these pieces seemed to grow from the nucleus of a theme (or even a single word) whose meanings needed to be unpacked. Verse is language put under such pressure that it emerges as some form of song, intensively; these pieces involved language being put into a thematic whole, extensively. The first activity, verse-making, is profoundly aesthetic; the second, prose-writing, is forensic. For all that, there were many places where the prose scalpel paused, as it were, and the improbable surgeon went off to have a cup of tea while humming, very gently, some relic of a half-forgotten tune.

And so, in the end, there it was: a typescript, tentatively called *Outside*. There were one or two other people – they're named in the 'Acknowledgements' at the back of the book – who took an interest in what I was doing, and their interest was equally kind and firm. I profited greatly from that interest and am deeply grateful for it. In a similar way, I'm grateful to the people, creatures, working rhythms and landscapes of this part of the Netherlands. Together with our neighbours I might admit the truth of the Dutch cliché *Er gaat niets boven Groningen* (ambiguous: 'Nothing beats Groningen' and/or

'There's nothing there, north of Groningen'). Held in that admission, I'm learning not to fret – not to fret too much – about whether or not I'm exiled; about where home might or might not be; and about whether or not I 'fit in'. *Outside* is, in its own way, a reply to those worries. It is, after all, like the abundant life from which it was generated, simply a way of happening.

Chris McCully
Usquert 2010

1

October 13th 2008
The roach-masters of Uithuizen

This week, the second week of October, the leaves on the garden trees have begun to fall. Every morning the blackbirds are busy in a lawn ever more strewn with tired yellow apple leaves. Spiders' webs in the corner of the lean-to next to the back garden are hung with dew and damp. The air smells of ploughing and silage, or is sharp with the after-taste of lime where the farmers have been trying, as they try every year, to enrich the sour heaviness of the Groningen clays. The roads running from the village into the polder are gobbed with mud thrown from the tread of tractor tyres.

It's time to go pike fishing. In years past I fished for pike as soon as the water temperatures came down to 20 degrees, and that meant fishing in September, which can be a good month for big fish. This year, hard pushed at work, I've hardly taken the pike rods from their tubes, though I comfort myself with the fact that the pike season ran traditionally from the beginning of October until the end of the following February. 'There's time,' I say aloud – though even as I reassure myself, I wonder, stranded here at fifty, how many more seasons I'll have left. There's time? 'There's time.' I say it anyway.

I made a kind of start yesterday, and made it by ignoring all the work there was to be done in the garden. I took down a light pike rod from its bracket, put a reel, some traces, a pair of unhooking pliers and a box of rubber shads in a shoulder bag, and set off to Uithuizen. It's in Uithuizen – a place uncertain whether it's a big village or a small town – that the canal called the Boterdiep ends. The Boterdiep – literally, the 'butter deep' – is so-called because it was once used to carry milk, cream and butter from these outlying farms and villages to the markets and the waiting ships in the city of Groningen. It's in Uithuizen that the canal has its northern terminus, and as it reaches it among the shops and shoppers, there's a road bridge and a small harbour. On the dock which runs along the eastern bank, elderly men sit with roach-poles. They catch roach, too – bright-scaled, handsome fish running to a pound or so, sometimes bigger. They expertly dismantle their poles while each fish is being played, swing the fish to hand, unhook it, slide it into a keepnet … and then the ritual of cigarette-making begins. Hands are dried on pieces of towel; weather-worn, work-roughened fingers dip into tobacco pouches; a film of paper is balanced, the leaf is spread… And all the while, out there in the harbour the little roach nitter at the surface. The paper is gummed. There's the tiny combustion of lighter; an aged head dips into a wisp of blue smoke. Then the pole is swung out again, and a pin-head-sized piece of pressed bread-flake is lowered to the reflection of the sky. Autumn clouds form and re-form around the luminous dot at the top of the float.

I'd often seen and admired them, the roach-fishers of Uithuizen. Sitting there on the dock, perched stiffly on their fishing baskets, they're the Dutch equivalents of Zen masters: they specialise in ritual patience and the stylised, skilled gesture. They're all, also, immensely old. The creases around their eyes have witnessed war, liberation and the difficult winters when, as boys, they fished for roach and killed them because they had to in order to supplement what would otherwise have been a diet as monotonous as the clay. They've been fishing ever since. The only difference is that these days they usually put the fish back.

Because the harbour in Uithuizen is a known roach-mark

I thought that the presence of these fish might attract their chief predator, the pike. I assembled the tackle by the roadside, climbed down a steep and muddy banking. Four Zen masters sat with roach-poles on the dock opposite me. One gestured, smiled. 'Gooi maar in,' he said. Just cast in.

There wasn't much room to cast the shad, given the presence of roach specialists on the far dock, shoppers on a near-side path, and a steep bank behind my head. I cast diagonally, letting the rubber fish sink to a metre, two metres. Then I worked back the lure so that it fluttered, dived, struggled upwards, sank again. I was trying to make the lure move like a crippled, dying roach. Nothing. Another cast, and ... again, nothing. A Zen master snapped his Zippo into life, purple cigarette smoke wreathed into a yellowed plane tree, and moments later a lorry braked at the road bridge in a roar of tyres.

I climbed back up the banking, slithered down again to where a willow was shedding crisp, curly leaves into a seam of very slow current under the bank. A row of wooden palings stretched away to my left at the edge of the water. I cast the shad again, closer to the bank this time, thinking that perhaps a pike might wait in ambush somewhere among the palings, watching the roach-shoals with cold, ancient eyes.

The shad was almost under my feet when the pike took. One moment I was watching the sunken undulations of the lure and its flash of red stripe; the next there was a rush of white-mottled flank, a snap of teeth and jaws, and the lure had been quickly and mercilessly inhaled.

The pike thrashed about on the surface, causing such a commotion that two workmen, who'd been fitting double-glazing to the front windows of a house on the other side of the road behind me, must have heard it, since they came across and gave a running commentary from some place just above my head. 'Hou 'm maar ...' Just hold him. Is he well hooked? Yes,

11

he's well hooked. He's going under that... No, he's out again.

Once it had got over its initial bout of head-shaking and surface-thrashing it was a remarkably well behaved pike. I drew it towards me. The big barbless single hook was fixed in the pike's lower jaw, and it was quick and easy work to slip the hook out with the pliers. The pike – a small fish of around 6lbs – steadied itself for a moment in the green, slow-moving surface, then sped away and down, back to its row of palings. It would be hunting again within the day.

'Didn't you want to take a photo?' asked the double-glazers. Conscious of the fact that I was being regarded by four pairs of ancient, roach-fishing eyes on the opposite bank I played nonchalant. 'Wat? Zo'n klein snoekje...?' What? With such a small pike? Buried inside the nonchalance, though, there was a certain unstated but fierce delight.

Leaves fell into gardens all over Groningen; blackbirds prised worms from moss; the shoppers went on with their weekend shopping; the roach-masters of Uithuizen paused to roll more tobacco ... and I'd caught the first pike of the autumn.

2

October 22nd 2008
The sex life of the freshwater mussel

People – English people – very occasionally ask me what a *polder* is. A Dutch polder is an area of farmland, typically land which has been reclaimed from water. The old method of draining the water was to pump it into a system of smaller or larger dykes which radiated outwards from the centre of the soon-to-be polder like the spokes of a lady's fan. At the circumference of the fan would be a much larger drainage canal, a *ringvaart*. Today, and particularly where the polder lies on peat or sand, the dykes run clear and are full of lilies and pondweed, which in turn harbours rudd and roach, who in turn attract pike. In truth, many polders could have been designed for pike fishing. We cast streamers over the serendipity of Dutch engineering.

Here in the north of Groningen the polders lie on clay, and some canals – in this dialect given their local name of *maren* – were constructed to follow the courses of old rivers, rivers which drained slowly over what was once a mosquito-infested marsh to the Wadden Sea. Many of the *maren*, therefore, including our local canal, the Usquerdermaar, meander quietly over the Groningen clays, and some are full of zander, a fish whose eyesight is apparently rather better adapted than the pike's to hunt in these turbid waters. But there are pike present, too, and sometimes they're very big fish.

In one reach of meanders within twenty minutes' walk of

where I'm writing these words the canal banks are in winter littered with the opened shells of freshwater mussels. The oystercatchers seem greedily fond of these muddy delicacies. There's a thin pearl sheen inside each newly opened shell – nacreous, cloud-reflecting. From an angling point of view the presence of these mussels means that the bit of the meander which they've colonised is likely to be a reach of canal favoured by predators, both zander and pike. I've sometimes puzzled about this, and once even suspected that the zander actually ate the mussels. These days I think it's far more likely that these mussel beds attract prey-fish such as tiny roach and sticklebacks, which in turn attract the zander and pike. Last year, for example, I caught a jack, a fish of around 5lbs, over one such mussel bed. As I prised the rubber shad out of the fish's jaw I found a dozen three-spined sticklebacks, some still alive, in the mouth cavity. Despite the fact that the pike had been predating on these tiny fish it had still had no problem whatsoever in turning its momentary rapacity on a lure six inches long. The same mark is also among the most productive on that reach of the *maar* for zander, which can sometimes run to 80cm, around 9 or 10lbs. I've even caught them there on the fly rods, since the water is sufficiently shallow (up to five feet deep) for fishing the streamer to be both efficient and effective.

The mussels I find here are duck mussels – that's *Anadonta anatina* to you. The rings on their outer shells are equivalent to tree- or scale-rings: the closely spaced rings, which show up as a dark streak on the outer shell, represent periods of minimal growth, ie. mostly in winter. Therefore you can tell the age of a mussel, albeit roughly (since mussels are also hugely responsive to any form of disturbance, and break out into rings at the drop of an oystercatcher's beak), by reading the rings on the carapace.

I hadn't realised that mussels can move themselves about underwater. I'd imagined that somehow they were fixed, like unpromising valves of muddy coral. A number of different sources, among them Macan and Worthington's *Life in Lakes and Rivers* (1972), instructed me differently, however. Mussels can in fact move about. They don't do so particularly quickly, and the speed at which they can travel is partly determined by the nature of the bottom across which they 'walk': this bottom is typically of sand or silt. Using an axe-shaped 'foot', which can be extended and retracted, they hudge through sludge. (The unworthy image I have is of an overweight man trying to climb a steep set of stairs using just his hands and arms: he … hudges … upwards.) The axe-shaped foot is also used to fix the mussel to the bottom where and whenever required.

The sources also speak eloquently of the mussels' function in the environments in which they're found – mussels are siphons, water-cleansers – and equally eloquently of the mussels' fascinating, if quiet, sex life. The female mussel, for instance, is fertilised by free-swimming sperm which enters her reproductive tract via that same siphon. The fertilised eggs develop into larvae which are kept in the female mussel's gills, living there in a waft of oxygenated water. (How efficient that mechanism is: the female mussel's very act of underwater breathing also serves to rear her own young.) Eventually, the mussel larvae exit their mother-host's gills and attach themselves to fish – I suspect, in our Dutch *maren* context, to zander. The host fish reacts to this act of parasitism by enclosing the mussel larvae in a cyst … which in rather less than a month, breaks free from the host, allowing the young mussels, once free of their host, to begin their lives in a different part of the canal or stillwater.

The English friends who occasionally visit us here sometimes come along on a walk, with or without a fishing rod, into the polder. To me, the polder's full of life – the hoarse, bizarre whistle of wigeon; curlews weeping in the emptied winter sky; grebes fishing down the edges of reed beds – and I'm beginning to be able to reconstruct some of what must be happening underwater. To our visitors, though, I suspect all that's visible is Dutch farmland, rain-glazed muddy fields stretching away to the curved horizon under the continual bleak winds. 'It's a bit … remote and austere, isn't it?' said one dear friend as he hugged himself into the warmth of his coat last January. But then I started trying to explain – about the clouds passing across the nacre of the opened mussel shell; about oystercatchers; and about zander who, it may be, unwittingly host exactly those features of the canal – the mussel beds – in and over which they will later hunt. Remote? Austere? It is beauty, and like the sex life of the freshwater mussel, it's constructed out of fish.

3

October 29th 2008
Bladderwrack and dulse

As I scrunched along the pebble beaches of Hindsholm on Funen, there in the heart of Denmark, it was the colours I noticed: the luminous greys of the storm-washed stones, the emerald greens of sea lettuce, the forest-green of eel-grass beds, and everywhere, dying seaweed and blown, drowned leaves. It was as if the autumnal landscape had become some sort of visual symphony – yellowing, falling birch leaves were a tremor on violins; the stricken umbers of horse chestnuts were a phrase on tubas; the oranges of the wind-torn dulse along the tideline were a long stave of cello music. It was the end of October. Sight had become sound. If Carl Nielsen had walked towards me carrying a sea-trout rod in one hand and a sheaf of manuscript paper in the other I wouldn't have been at all surprised.

It's not for nothing that the Danes call the sea-trout 'the fish of a thousand casts'. While I fished out my dutiful thousand at Tårup, and then another weary thousand or two at Lundsgård and Bøgebjerg, I found my concentration wandering in the direction of the seaweed on the beach and the weed whose structure felt so pliable against the felt soles of my waders. Someone, I thought, should write about the angling importance of the different kinds of seaweed. After all, many anglers are today familiar, if only from their reading, with the importance of ranunculus and other plants to the chalkstream fly-fisher, and august chapters in even more august books are filled with tussles among tresses, with the significance of weed-cutting, and with the gigantic trout, soon to be lost, that weeds the angler decisively. We're also familiar with the insects that tend to colonise or favour the chalkstream plants (I thought, as I cast for the thousand-and-first time towards a grey scurry of westerly on the surface twenty yards away). And yet of the coastal and estuarial plants we, as anglers, generally read little and equally generally, know less.

Then I realised that I myself knew virtually nothing of the seaweeds – nothing of their etymologies, their evolutionary history, nor of the creatures who favour them as habitats.

Standing there in body waders, in sea water whose temperature was shooting down from 11°C to 9°C, I peered towards my submerged feet. Waving in the current were long filaments of weed – thongweed, I learned later, and a plant (said Peter Hayward's *Seashore*) which was not to be muddled up with 'mermaid's tresses'. What were mermaid's tresses? I kept my eyes open for a plant whose tendrils looked like the aftermath of a drowning – and there, left of me at Tårup, was *Chorda filum*, though the corpse in question could have used a good dose of biological shampoo. There, too, was a kind of wrack. Spiral Wrack it was, *Fucus spiralis*. And there, another kind of wrack, this one having pairs of gas bladders arranged symmetrically up its leaves. That's bladderwrack, or *Fucus vesiculosus* to you.

I wondered why the bladderwrack had bladders. What do they do, these bladders? I mulled while I made the three thousand and twenty-first cast in the general direction of an island in the far distance. I didn't know. Why should a leaf have bladders? Leaves on trees don't have bladders, so why should seaweeds…? Then I arrived at a kind of answer. The leaves of the bladderwrack have bladders because the bladders help the leaves of the plant to float. And why should the leaves of this particular seaweed be adapted to float? So they can catch any available sunlight. *That's* why. (I silently added the word 'stupid' there – That's why, stupid.) Photosynthesis. Ah. Of course.

While the maddened, autumnal percussions of Nielsen symphonies boomed in the back of my head, the front of it was filled with an amateur's engagement with the opportunistic behaviour of the various seaweeds. Yes, it had come to that: a middle-aged man pondering the angling significance of sea beads, wracks, knotweed, sea-oaks and the Orange Encrusting Sponge. Apart from anything else it was simply the names of these plants that I found, and still find, so entrancing. Some talented poet should one day try to do some justice to this venerable, deeply embedded strand of the English lexicon. *Purple Laver, Red Rags, Furbelows* and *Oarweed*. You relish them even as you pronounce them.

As for the creatures which live in these weeds, then it seems clear that shrimps and prawns find eel-grass beds much to their liking; isopods of different kinds – those adapted to crawl among fronds rather than burrow – seem to like tangles of wrack; sandhoppers appear to love dulse; crabs colonise everything. It seemed no accident that the last sea-trout I'd killed on the Funen coasts, a fish of just over the size limit of 40cm, had had a small crab, various isopods and the remains of a shrimp in its guts. It had taken the fly in a sheltered part of the Odense fjord, among mussel beds and generous spreads of horned wrack.

I'd reached the words 'horned wrack' when – on merely the four thousand and eighth cast – a sea-trout took. I was so shocked I did nothing except arc the rod involuntarily. There was a swirl along the outer edge of a line of floating thongs of ... of thongweed. Birch leaves frittered down the end of a squall – more violins, a tremolo – and somewhere far off there was the endless double-bass sough of the first big westerly storm of the coming winter.

I played the fish out of the orchestra of sea and weather, steered it out of the thongweed, drew it to hand. It was a typical autumn sea-trout, 'going back' as anglers say – that is, the fish was in the process of losing the bright silver of its summer scales and was showing the duller spawning livery underneath. I slipped out the hook, cradled the fish upright above the tendrils of weed. One flare of its gills, and it sped away, back to the edge of the reef and all its winter journeys.

It was to be almost the last sea-trout of this season. After enduring there on Hindsholm through four days of gales I reeled in past sunset on Bøgebjerg Strand, crunched carwards over pebbles. The sun left a wiped yellow stain on the western sky. It was cloudless, and early cold. How many thousand casts? Four thousand? Five? The question started to line up rhythmically with the bite of wading boots on beach: five-*thous*and-casts-and-*dulse*; five-*thous*and-casts-and-*dulse*; *bladder*wrack and *saw*-toothed wrack – and *dulse*, dulse, *dulse*.

4

November 6th 2008
The adventures of a leaf

Like the rest of the northern European world – at least, that part of the world equipped with brushes, shovels and leaf-blowers – I've spent odd hours during the past week raking the lawn clear of apple, plum and variegated maple leaves. As I raked and brushed a question began to form among the minor human rhythms of autumn clearing: why do leaves decompose? That question brought with it some supplementaries: why do leaves change colour? Why are some autumn leaves red, while others are yellow? Why is a leaf generally flat?

Leaves are flat because a flat structure maximally exposes the cells of a leaf to sunlight. Within the leaf cells are units called chloroplasts, which are the stars of the piece when it comes to photosynthesis. In photosynthesis, the leaves of a tree absorb light and use it, together with water and carbon dioxide, to produce oxygen and sugar. In other words, while the tree is breathing (via the leaf system) it is also producing energy, which then helps the tree to survive and grow. During this process, leaves are green because the chlorophyll molecules bonded to the chloroplasts absorb light in such a way that their pigmentation shows as … well, as green. Because the chlorophyll molecules are particularly active in spring and summer, their abundance, activity and sheer greenness masks

20

the colour-presence of other molecules in structure of the leaf. Some of these other molecules are carotenoids, and these may appear brown or yellow. In autumn, as the chlorophyll supply in each leaf declines, the browns and yellows of the carotenoids become more visible. In trees whose leaves seem to turn red in the autumn, this redness is caused by another group of molecules, anthocyanins, which are created as the phosphate levels in the structure of the leaf reduce.

As light levels drop in the autumn, photosynthesis decreases. The tree produces fewer sugars and generates less energy. Once this happens, the cells which help to connect the leaf to its stem are weakened. Eventually, the leaf detaches from the stem.

Further, just suppose a deciduous tree attempted to retain its leaves during the winter. It would be a radically profligate and expensive strategy, since the very flatness of its leaves, which proved so useful during the summer, would be a liability in winter, since the veins containing the sap would be maximally exposed to frost. And again, attempting to keep flat-structured foliage alive during the winter would require more energy than was stored in the tree: the tree would die as a consequence of trying to stay alive. Far more efficient, therefore, for deciduous trees to become dormant in the frosts and relative darkness of winter.

Decomposition continues once the leaf is detached from the structure of the tree. Bacteria, parasites, insects, earthworms: they eat through what's left of the dead leaf, while the leaf literally breathes its last as any remaining organic material breaks down into water and carbon dioxide. Eventually, what is left is a trace of CO_2, the hint of a water droplet, extruded particles in the soil.

As I raked and brushed I thought about those leaf particles. I imagined a speck of dust lying there under the undone maple in the garden. It would possibly find its way, via my brush and shovel, into the local council's recycling unit, and from there into the nearby canal. There, perhaps, it might settle, and make the ten trillionth fragment of a metre of silt ... out of which, in turn, water plants might grow. Or perhaps, having found its way into the canal, it would be pumped seawards – only to find itself being recycled inside the cavernous shell of the freshwater mussel. Or again, having accidentally evaded the mussel, it might eventually wash through sluices, brickwork and the slow tides, into the remote spaces of the Wadden Sea. It would be covered by flatfish; be ingested by brit and then travel through summer mackerel; migrate into hosts. It could possibly find itself falling into the cold darkness at the edge of the trenches which are gouged by time and volcanoes into the floors of the deep oceans. Alternatively, it could fetch up far from here in the quiet and almost tideless, pike-infested bays of the northerly Baltic, where it would become the host for the stem of a plant which in turn hosted the insects eaten by grayling.

I paused with the rake. Three gardens away, one of our

neighbours had switched on his leaf-blower. The afternoon whined electronically with evening and the first week of November. I looked at the diminishing pile of leaf litter and debris lying on the paving by the sundial in front of me.

'I have no idea' – I said to this unpromising heap of incipient water and dust – 'where you'll end up.' The low sun shouldered up the edge of a cloud and, late in the day, red-gold light touched the top of the sails of the village windmill.

No, I have no idea – and equally, have little idea whether leaf fall, once it finds its way into streams, lakes and canals, somehow sickens the fish. Reg Righyni mentions that late October and early November leaf fall can put the grayling briefly off the feed (*Grayling*, p.69), and I can't see why this wouldn't be the case.

I brushed the last of the heap into the shovel, shook it into the recycling bin. It will become smaller; its constituents will travel; far from anywhere, this handful of leaf litter will be continually reused. Suddenly, from the debris which composes the future and nowhere, there came the mental image of the maw of the oyster, filaments of weed streaking the serrations of the outer shell, a speck of grit.

As light failed across the cobbles and became a darkening mist in monochrome, autumn became a pearl.

5

November 10th 2008
Harbours and kingfishers

As the foliage in the garden dies and the leaves fall, the resident birds become more visible. Two robins follow my fork and the autumn digging. Though both birds will approach

23

closely to the tines and the newly turned soil, they nevertheless keep a wary distance from each other, and occasionally, one will chase the other away. For a second or two a yard of air hurtles with indignant wings and screams. Meanwhile, two wrens are busy in the thinning hedge which surrounds the lawn; blue tits, great tits, chaffinches and greenfinches are busy at the three feeders hanging from the lower boughs of the apple tree; and blackbirds – alert, dangerous – stalk earthworms in the grass.

Later autumn and winter are a good time of year to watch resident birds. Two days ago, walking back from an afternoon spent out in the polder trying to catch zander on softbaits, I was surprised again by the kingfisher which lives and hunts in Usquert harbour. During the winter I see this bird very often. It sits motionless on one of the branches that overhang the far bank, or aims up- or downwind past the moored boats, uttering its single-noted, monotonous, twice-repeated 'tschek, tschek'. Clearly the bird is hunting the tiny roach and rudd fry which are the progeny of this summer's spawning – they have gathered into tight-knit shoals lying in sheltered water by this time of year – or perhaps it's predating on the sticklebacks to which the Usquerdermaar is also host.

For a description of the hunting behaviour of the kingfisher there's no better than that of that great angler and naturalist W.H. Hudson: 'Day after day it returns to the same perch, where it sits watching the surface, silent and immovable as a heron. It looks out for its prey both when perched and when flying at a height of a few feet above the surface, and often hovers motionless for a few moments before darting down into the water. With the minnow it captures held crossways in its beak it flies to a perch and, after beating it against the branch or stone, swallows it, head first, sometimes tossing it in the air and catching it as it falls' (*British Birds*, 1902, p.189).

24

I wondered briefly why kingfishers were called kingfishers. I had some dim idea that 'king' referred to their royally capable manner of fishing (in the same way as 'king' refers to the royally generous dimensions of a kingsize bed) but the *Oxford English Dictionary* (OED), which I consult about most things, told me differently. The OED notes that the kingfisher was also referred to as the Halcyon bird – a bird of fables which was allegedly bred at the winter solstice 'in a nest floating on the sea … [I]t charmed the wind and waves so that the sea was specially calm during this period; usually identified with the kingfisher…' Thus the Halcyon, a word first attested in 1390 in John Gower's *Confessio Amantis*. (The ancient association of the bird with winter might also help to account for the Dutch name for the bird: *ijsvogel* – 'ice-bird'. Happily, too, and although several Dutch natural history guides note that the *ijsvogel* is 'zeldzaam bij ons' – rare in the Netherlands – its numbers here seem to be increasing, probably as a result of year-on-year improvements to water quality in the freshwater systems of all the Dutch provinces.)

Of the kingfisher itself, then nesting there between *king-fish* and *king-head* is the entry for *Alcedo ispida*. In that entry, the OED notes 'the belief that a dried specimen hung up indicated by its position the direction in which the wind was blowing'. The first attestation of the word *kingfisher* comes – rather late in terms of the history of the English language – in 1440: 'Kyngys fyschare, lyttyle byrde'.

It interests me somewhat that the 1440 writer uses the suffix –ys: *kyng+ys*. This isn't a misprint, but represents what we'd now write as apostophe+s: *king's*. *King's+fisher*. Presumably, the bird is thus called either because kings liked to be associated with fabulous creatures, or – and perhaps more plausibly – liked to impress with their apparent powers of divination during the winter solstice. Moreover, if the winter solstice was a time of calm weather, then fishing fleets could put to sea, and any resulting catch could be credited to the intervention of that pathetic scrap of stiff electric-blue feathers with the awesomely predictive powers of the sovereign. *Cry God for Harry, halcyons and herrings*!

Whatever its fabulous etymological and regal origins, the kingfisher has spectacularly filthy habits. Hudson again: 'The kingfisher, like the owl and cuckoo and many other species, casts up the indigestible portions of its food – the minute bones of minnows in this case – in the form of small pellets. The pellets are thrown up into the nest chamber, and, when broken up and pressed down by the sitting-bird, are shaped into a cuplike nest' (1902, p.189). The nest itself is usually sited within a bankside hole which may be between one to four feet deep. Very many years ago, when I was still impatiently small, I discovered such a nest – and withdrew a grit-covered woollen sleeve at the end of which was a boy's hand sticky with fish-offal and utterly repulsive to smell for hours afterwards.

The kingfisher also brings with it the purely private lexicon of friendship. With the books and illustrations lying open on the study table I thought back to the evenings on the Wharfe at Kilnsey when Bill and I often saw one, sometimes two kingfishers as we set off towards Mile House Dub to try and catch brown trout at twilight and beyond. Crunching up the river's edge on the gravel, we'd always be delighted, and always pause for a moment to watch that impossible, dead straight bolt of orange-hinted turquoise. And then, with a feeling of having been touched by some beneficent strangeness, we'd get on with the blue-winged olives, and then sedges as the last light finally failed, and then big wake-flies in the full darkness. It makes me smile, now, from this distance of time and harbours, to think that those were quite literally halcyon evenings.

6

November 16th 2008
The names of the Pleiades

One of the strange and lovely things about being outside and keeping your eyes open is that the very act of looking connects you with the earlier self who was you, when you also looked at the same things or looked at them in similar contexts. In that awareness, even the most apparently casual glance is also full of fragments of personal history. The eyes which are you are memory.

During the past week we've had some clear nights when the world has been cast in what has almost been frost; nights when the floodlit spire of Usquert church, sited five hundred yards away to the east, has locked itself into sharp-etched winter shadows; nights when the great winter constellations appear to wheel upwards from the Dollard estuary and then drift high and south. Among these constellations is the group of cosmologically young stars which everyone knows as the Pleiades.

Some constellations, the Pleiades among them, aren't visible in the summer from the northern hemisphere. That's because when the world turns it also wobbles on its axis, rather like the gyrations of an exhausted top. When this hemisphere tilts towards the sun, the result is the longer or shorter northern summer; when this hemisphere is tilted away from the sun, the result is winter – and the appearance of those constellations invisible in summer (because at that time these same constellations lie below our horizon). Among these constellations are Taurus (which hosts the Pleiades) and Orion, both instantly recognisable, both dominating the southern sky, and both excellent markers for orientating the eye to other constellations elsewhere in the heavens.

Each time I see the Pleiades rising over the spire of the church I try to count them. On any moderately clear night I can usually count four or five. On exceptionally clear nights I can sometimes count (or think I can count) six. They are all blue stars – still millions of years young, and still burning with blue intensity, unlike the older stars which are collapsing into the red heat of their own age and immensity, and appear yellow, amber or even amber-red. That said, the assumption that 'blue stars are young, red stars old' is over-simple. Betelgeuse, for example – there it is on Orion's shoulder – is apparently even younger that the Pleiades, but is a red giant even to the naked eye, largely because it's so huge and so fast-burning that it has already consumed itself. It's dying even as we look at it – but even then, what we're actually looking at is Betelgeuse as it was 10 million years ago, since that's how long its dying light has taken to reach us. Before any clocks or telescopes, even before there were any human eyes, what travelled down the darkness was still time.

The Pleiades are also known as the Seven Sisters, who derive from Greek mythology, where the Seven Sisters – Alcyone, Electra, Merope, Maia, Asterope, Celaeno, Taygeta – were the daughters of Atlas and Pleione, from which mythical lady the sisters perhaps drew their collective name. (Atlas was one of the original Titans, later condemned by Zeus to eternal punishment which comprised holding the spheres of the heavens on his shoulders.) It's also thought that the term 'Pleiades' might just derive from the Greek verb *pleion* 'to sail', since the Seven Sisters are visible at night in the Mediterranean. They are the sailing stars.

Even on the clearest night I can rarely count seven of the Seven Sisters. Perhaps that's because the seventh of the Seven

Sisters was allegedly kidnapped by one of the Seven Brothers whose lights make up Ursa Major (which I was raised to call 'the Plough'). If that's true, you can look for her adjacent to the star called Mizar, the next-to-last star of the 'handle' of the Plough, whose ploughshare startles what Arab astronomers saw as three gazelles – three groups of two stars, each group lying below the Plough's gigantic blade.

The Pleiades form part of the constellation called Taurus, the bull against whose imaginary rush Orion extends his shield. In this galactic frieze Orion, the hunter, is accompanied by two dogs – Canis Major (who runs at his feet) and Canis Minor (who jumps at his shoulder). Dogs, gazelles, sisters, hunter and bull: there in the winter sky an ancient cosmic drama plays itself out – endless, voiceless, motionless. Nothing is ever quite the same, but nothing ever changes. I watch anyway.

I watch anyway, because every way I watch helps to join me up. I first became aware of Orion, for instance, while I was walking south towards Cashel in Connemara in 1976. It was a bitter March night, and I'd been given a lift to the junction at Recess. From there a single-track road runs south over the bog towards Cashel before turning west and down to the coast. From that perspective, on the road running south, I guessed that Sirius, the brightest star in the night sky, lay more or less directly over the cottage. That is, while I knew the names of some constellations, back then in 1976, that small foot journey was the first time I'd been able to use them as orientational markers for a local purpose – much as the boat-fisherman uses a tree, hill or mountain peak to align his way up the lough to the start of a new drift. And meanwhile, as I walked, I dreamed of the fish I would catch that year, and the following day walked back up the same road and caught a little wild brown trout from Lough Lurgainn on a Mallard and Claret. That first trout of the season was a gift from Sirius, whose apparent location in Atlantic space had marked the end of a difficult trip.

There was another night, too, almost two decades later. I had been fishing for early sea-trout in the Till. Again it was a bitter March. I had caught nothing, but had persisted into twilight, and even beyond. It was low water, frost-clear. The evening was utterly windless. In the slow glass of pool-tails I watched the trees become angles of darkness past which the constellations rose, and fished on so long and hopelessly that I was eventually casting a size 4 blue-and-silver Mepps upstream and retrieving it, spellbound, through all the Pleiades.

7

November 24th 2008
The village named by fish

The names of many villages in this part of the Netherlands end on the syllable written *–um* (pronounced '-em'): Rottum, Warffum, Middelstum. That's not too hard to work out: *-um* is similar to, and cognate with, what fetches up in English as *–ham* (also pronounced '-em'): Cookham, Fordham, Addingham, where *–ham* represents 'farm, homestead'. Yet *Usquert* – the name of the village where we live – looks graphologically odd by any West Germanic standards. The main curiosity is formed by the <q>. If you – wrongly, as it will turn out – allow the <q> to begin the second syllable of the name – *Us+quert* – then you begin to ask yourself what an *Us* might have been. A year ago, before we moved to het Hogeland, I dimly imagined that 'Us' might have been related to the root *os-*, and have been something to do with bones (Latin *ossa*, compare English *ossuary*, ?present-day Dutch place-name *Osdorp*, ?the village of bones). But here, as so often elsewhere, my dim imaginings turned out merely to be fictions. I was wrong.

To understand the origins of the name it's necessary to reconstruct what this northerly coastline looked like twelve hundred years ago. At present, the coast begins a couple of miles north of this desk, which is separated from the sea by three dykes. In the 9th century, however, this village lay on the coast. The land that lies north of us, all clay and potato drills, has been slowly reclaimed from the Wadden Sea.

To the south of us, and inland, lie villages which have always been non-coastal, and which furthermore have been even longer settled. The first, pre-Christian inhabitants apparently came from what is now the province of Drenthe, prospecting north to the coast in order to find rich grazing land for their cattle. Further, some of the first written records of the Christianisation of this part of the Low Countries relate to the conversion of the poet, Bernlef, by the Frisian apostle Liudger in the 8th and early 9th centuries. Liudger was by no means some hopeless, dirty, eschatalogically minded vagabond, but had received instructions from Charlemagne himself. As it happened, Bernlef was blind, and was unable to see his beloved village of Warffum (a village which lies three miles west of Usquert). Endowed with the divine gift of healing, Liudger completed a miraculous cure, with the result that Bernlef was once again able to see his home. Bernlef was subsequently instructed by the itinerant preacher to compose verse witnessing to the miracle and praising his Ultimate Healer. And after such sterling work here in het Hogeland, Liudger was appointed Bishop of Munster in 804. The same story plays itself out, with minor variations, in many of the northern Germanic cultures and literatures – not so much because northern Europe was strewn with blind poets but largely, one suspects, because it

31

suited early Christian propagandists to insist that the new faith brought spiritual as well as literal clear-sightedness.

Whatever the small divine drama completing itself at Helwerd, a hamlet whose roofs I can almost see as I write, in the 9th century our fragment of this northerly coastline ran from Warffum through Usquert to Uithuizen (literally, the 'outer houses'). The shore is a sort of slow, fastidious, north-bulging curve. It's no accident that to your immediate left as you drive from west to east past Warffum, Usquert, and into Uithuizen there are the remains of an ancient dyke: the *Oudendijk*. This once marked the transition between farmland and the mud flats of a midge- and disease-infested Wadden whose shallow tides sucked then, as now, at mud.

Let's stay with the local topography of the 9th century for a moment longer. Back then, slow-flowing creeks bisected the flat lands close to the coast. Some ran north-easterly, meandering over the marsh; others ran westerly, towards what is now the Lauwersmeer. Later, after the land had been drained and new canals constructed, the new canals were in places made to follow the courses of the old creeks, with the result that our present-day canals here and there still contain the ancient meanders. Where one can find these bends they are invariably good places to fish for pike and zander, which tend to lie either on the inside of a bend, or in the straight piece of canal either side of a bend (from which lie they predate into the bend itself).

Therefore, when one thinks back twelve hundred years, Usquert was surrounded by fish: there in the muds of the Wadden were flatfish and eels; in the brackish creeks south of the village were pike, zander, eels and perch.

It's the fish connection which helps to explain the etymology of the name. Present-day Usquert was once 'Visc' (pronounced with a final 'k' – *fisk*) and 'wierd' or 'werd', pronounced *vurt*. And what is a *w(i)erd*? It's another sort of dyke, composed out of fish scraps, bones, household refuse, offal. *Viskwerd* – the place of the fish dyke. What's in a *vurt*?

In the 14th century another, more northerly sea dyke was begun. That now lies a mile north of this desk. The original Oudendijk thereafter became redundant, or if not completely redundant, assumed a status as a sort of back-up dyke which might function if – heaven forbid – the new dyke was breached. And in the 18th century yet another new sea dyke was completed. That one lies just south of the present-day coastline, and that one, likewise, made the 14th century dyke redundant, unless the unthinkable happened and the Wadden roared through or over the later dyke, stranding sole, turbot and plaice in the new potato fields.

I'd got this far in my very minor piece of etymological detective work when in a 20th-century village annual I came across the coat-of-arms (Dutch *wapen*) of Usquert. This comprises two fish which are set vertically and symmetrically either side of a sprinkle of three Maltese crosses. The fish look like stylised, prancing whiting to me, and the Maltese crosses symbolise a local cloister (the *Wijtwerdklooster*), a religious house which once, according to all records, was stupendously rich, no doubt on the proceeds of fish. The cloister was closed in 1618. A large farm now stands on the spot, just south of the Usquerdermaar.

WAPEN VAN USQUERT

On the *Landschappelijke karakteristiek* (topography) page of this village's web pages (http://www.usquert.nl/oud/) the first paragraph begins with the sentence 'Usquert has always been closely connected with the sea'. It makes me smile, to think that of all the places in the world at which I could have ended I have ended – or at least, paused for a while – in a village constructed out of rubbish, conditioned by the myths of religion, and named by fish.

8

1st December 2008
On not loving zander

Over the past few years I've tried hard to love zander. I've failed. Over the same period it was pike which, if they did not quite steal my angling heart, yet compelled my respect. Nevertheless, zander are not only widespread in the Netherlands, but abundant in this part of the country – in het Hogeland, where reed-fringed, murk-carrying canals large and small thread through ploughed riggs and old hubs of villages to the mudflats of the Wadden Sea.

I suppose I was spoiled while we lived south of Amsterdam. Within a half-hour's drive were clearwater lakes whose shallows were riddled with pondweed, and polders cut from peat and sand whose canals and pools were, likewise, weed-infested and full of interest. Even the cuts and canals which ran through resolutely urban and suburban places usually ran clear – clear enough so that you could feasibly fish a streamer and (crucially) have the confidence that a watching pike would be able to see it. To ply the 9-weight and watch the big streamer

34

pulsing there towards the end of the retrieve... To see the streamer annexed by a sudden flash of olive-mottled flank... To feel the line draw away into the last of winter, and to feel the winter live with the weight of pike... I loved that, and loved it all the more for the fact that it was so surprising. Occasionally, having caught, say, three or four pike, of an average weight of 5-6lbs, during the course of a February afternoon with the fly-rods, I used to remind myself that if, for instance, I'd fished Chew Valley Lake for trout and had ended the afternoon with a leash of similar-sized fish I'd have thought I'd had a wonderful time.

One of the reasons I enjoyed that pike fly-fishing so much was that the waters generally were clear. Sunlight could penetrate into the shallows, and accordingly, the shallows hosted the weed beds in and around which the pike would lie. True, in the very depths of winter the pike tended to lie as deep as possible, in sudden holes and sullen spreads of ink-grey, remote water. At those times they would take a static deadbait better than any moving lure. Still, towards the end of January and through February back the pike would come, as their spawning instincts urged them to seek out the shallows once more. I would find the pike then among the dead weed beds of the previous year – blackened shreds of water lilies; brown, fungal strands of pondweed; the stubs and shards of iris… In these promising places, in what was often the bitterest of weather, I could often follow the course of the streamer on the retrieve and in turn, enjoy the shocking, slow-motion hurtle of that cream-green, thumb-printed wide flank as the pike turned onto the streamer fishing, wavering a foot down in the winter water.

The canals in this part of the country have a different character. They're usually cut into mud and clay, and they're rarely clear enough for fly-fishing to be feasible. Further, such relatively murky waters suit zander rather better than pike. Zander, after all, have eyes which are adapted to predate best in low-light conditions, and generally speaking, zander prefer to use the security of depth and bottom contours, rather than the shelter of weed beds, as places from which to hunt – not that there are many weed beds in our local canals. They seem to lie, too, around bream shoals and mussel beds. Last year, therefore, soon after we'd moved, and as I tried to come to terms with a strange and silly feeling of what was almost disappointment, I pulled out the multiplier, exhumed the two-piece light pike rods, and put some softbaits and rattle-plugs into the lure-box. I prospected the drop-offs, the edges of reed beds; areas inside and outside canal bends haunted by grebes and cormorants; harbours and junctions. For every pike I caught last season here in het Hogeland I must have caught three zander, and almost all of them came on softbaits, the 6-inch Mann's shad (flavour: Pepper) preeminent among them.

Just occasionally, however – windless days after frost; calm, rainless spells which allow the waters to drop and settle – it's possible to fish the streamer. Underwater visibility still isn't good, but it's sufficient for the zander to be able to sight the fly as it rocks there at the edges of drop-offs on the retrieve. I'm lucky that I can find zander at all in the heart of winter. On many waters, zander lie very deep throughout the coldest months – too deep for fishing with the fly rods, even where these are equipped with Hi-D or lead-cored lines. It simply takes too long to wait for the line and streamer to sink to what is often 10 or even 20 metres. Far more effective to use a softbait, and, from bank or boat, to jig it across the bottom. In the local canal, however, the deepest the zander can go is around nine feet, and sometimes, particularly as February progresses into March, they can be so apparently aggressive that they'll take a streamer fished a mere three or four feet below the surface.

I can't claim to have caught hundreds of zander on the fly rods, but over the course of the past year I suppose I must have caught a score, all on 8-weight gear and an intermediate line. The streamer has invariably been a Flash Fly, size range 2- 4/0, usually including an epoxy head constructed over a pair of stick-on, extra-large eyes. The weight of the epoxy head helps the tinsels in the rest of the pattern to flare enticingly during short pulls on the retrieve, and perhaps I should stress that I do retrieve the streamer slowly, in 6-inch pulls, allowing it time to sink and flare before repeating the process.

The take of a zander to the streamer is rather unlike that of a pike. Pike will follow – will *stalk* – the streamer, then at the last moment open their cavernous mouths and literally suck the streamer in … whereupon it's held and caught by all those backward-raking, vicious-looking teeth. What you feel in the line is, often enough, a shocking jolt. Zander, on the other hand, rise quickly from the bottom and seem to snap at the streamer, meaning that what you feel in the line is often no more than a flaccid bump.

Therefore when I have to scratch the itch to use the fly rods again, and so long as the canals remain reasonably clear, I take out the 8-weight and throw a streamer at zander. I appreciate they're wonderfully handsome fish – gold-olive scaled, wild, full-finned and bristling with power. I've even caught one or two quite big ones on the fly rods, the largest of them to date 8½lb, and the one zander I've killed tasted magnificent (and surprisingly delicate) when cooked with a mustard sauce. Yet for all their abundance, their weight on the rod, their edibility and the intricacy and interest of their habits… Many people love them; and somehow, I cannot.

9

8th December 2008
On the border of loneliness

One of the things that often surprises me is the subtle difference in the landscapes of two adjacent Dutch provinces. Here in the north of Groningen, for instance, the land is resolutely clay and spuds. Plane tree and poplar skirt the edges of endless potato drills. The canals are full of suspended mud. Just thirty kilometres to the south, however, lies sand and peat. Sheep overwinter in the fields between knots of ash, willow and silver birch. The canals are choked with weed – *boterbloem* and *dotterbloem*, water buttercup and marsh marigold – and carry peat-stain. This landscape begins just south of the city of Groningen, and extends south and west through the county of Drenthe.

Of all Dutch provinces, Drenthe reminds me of what 18th-century Norfolk or Suffolk must have been like. Between the stands of silver birches lies wonderful shooting country and the civilised spaces of what another age might have called Gentleman's Estates. The farmhouses are more like small stately homes than farms, and it seems no accident that one of the larger canals that runs east-north-east through Drenthe towards Groningen is called the Jonkersvaart, since a *jonker* was, Kramer's Dutch-English dictionary tells me, a 'country squire' (cf. German *junker*). An English intelligence half expects to see Thomas Gainsborough fiddling about with his easel, and Mr. and Mrs. Andrews posing somewhat stiffly for an eternal posterity under their oak tree. It all seems so ... English, and in the landscape-painting context it seems to be no accident that Gainsborough (1727-1788) was born in Suffolk, and worked for several years in Ipswich, where his clientele included 'local squires'. The two landscapes – those of Suffolk, and those of parts of the northern Netherlands – of course have much in common, even to the dykes and the expertise which built them.

I hadn't fished the Jonkersvaart before, and a first glance wasn't altogether encouraging. The weed-cutting machines had clearly been at work, and on each bank of the canal were piled large heaps of water buttercup and marigold stalks. As I stared squirishly – a squire of no name and of nothing – at the mist dissolving over the grey winter surface of the water I wondered briefly whether to drive on, or back, or simply to go home. Then, below a lock, where the fall of the sluice-current smoothed into a trickle of calm-water foam, I caught the dimple of a rising roach. Then another. In oily water backed up above the sluice I saw a curious and miniature seething in the surface which could only be that of a little perch avid on pin-fry. The small fish, therefore, were awake, and feeding, and where there is an abundance of small fish, and sufficient depth in which to hunt and to rest, then there, of course, will be the winter pike.

I tackled up with a smallish shad and a 7g jig-hook. As I was threading the braid through the rings I kept thinking about Gainsborough, about Mr. and Mrs. Andrews, and about the empty space left by the artist there in Mrs. Andrews' lap. What was the space destined to be filled by? Book? Bible? Fruit? A brace of grouse?

A pike hit on the second cast ... and somehow, fell off. A wan sun brightened on the white striations of the bark of silver birches on the far bank. Five hundred yards behind me, a tractor coughed massively into life from the stink of silage. Fifty yards away a man was raking blackened leaves from his lawn. After the tractor had woken, roared and gone I could hear the tines scratching at frozen earth. Five yards away there was another heap and ton of marigold stems to navigate. Another pike hit … and promptly fell off. It came again on the next cast, too … and fell off again.

Ten minutes' fishing; three pike moved. I changed the lure, replaced the trailing treble with a smaller treble. I cast again into the channel where the little roach were still occasionally dimpling. I hooked another pike. It thrashed momentarily in the surface – a flash of jaw and gills in peat-stained water … and it dropped off.

It's at moments like this that I would often like to have some angling company. To move, hook and drop four pike in succession is fairly remarkable, particularly when you're fishing with soft-baits, whose very softness and collapsibility minimises bulk and leverage when a pike strikes, and which therefore hook pike reliably … usually. And there on the Jonkersvaart, where the usual had just become the balefully remarkable, it would have been good to have someone there with whom … to whom …

There was nobody. Even the man raking leaves had gone inside for a mug of coffee and a *koekje*. There was the noise of the fall of the sluice, and beyond that, merely the cold ball of a smeared winter sun and a huge and birdless silence.

In a monochrome world I changed the lure again. This one had just a wickedly sharp single hook. I walked ten yards, to where a trickle of water leaked into the canal from a field drain. I cast – and hooked another pike. This one played deep. I had it on long enough so that I had time to work out where on the bank I could safely unhook it. The pike clearly must have read my mind, in which it saw the word 'Hubris'. This pike, too, dropped off.

Yes, I thought, it would have been good if there had been someone here to … But what would I have said? And what could they have said? I don't know, but sometimes even a wordless company, out there in the zeros of winter, is better than no company at all.

As it was, there was Gainsborough, and the depth and interest of the imaginative landscape in which I'd just become a ... no, not a squire, but rather some minor 18th-century local clergyman, indulging his hobby in a chastened, sober, Christian seclusion...

I hooked another pike. It fell off. I changed the lure again; sharpened the hook.

...respected by his parishioners... enthusiastic amateur member of ... known and respected for his scientific work on the naming and collection of different kinds of seaweeds...

(I hooked another.)

...Corresponding Member of the Royal Society... handshakes at Christmas under the church porch... ivy and burials...

(.)

...And there in Drenthe I came to another kind of border, a baffled parenthesis, a civilised space filled by winter and the memory of an 18th century English painting, by pike I couldn't hook, and by something I could identify neither as loneliness nor as happiness.

10

20th December 2008
Manic fly-tying

Once, when the world was younger, I had one fly-box – a small aluminium Wheatley whose leaves held fifty-one clips (which I have, sadly, just counted). This original – the Ur-fly-box, as it were – was the size of a slim cigarillo tin. Now the world is older and more beaten up I have twenty-six fly-boxes and wallets, and that total doesn't count the row of barbless pike Bunnies (6/0) which are at this moment pinned to the cork board behind my head. Nor, come to think of it, does it include the boxful of dapping flies. Nor the dozen sea-trout tandems drying in a block of ethafoam on the work bench. Nor the streamers in the wallet in the pocket of my fishing waistcoat.

Even I recognise this as something verging on the ridiculous, if not the mad. The irony is that these days I tend to tie flies for friends and acquaintances rather than for my own, already over-ample stock. I give away far more than I use, or will ever use. I still have twenty-six fly-boxes.

Occasionally I ask myself whether fly-tying, which tends to occupy the winter months, has become a form of addiction. I suppose, and suppose ruefully, that it has – not because the purchase of feathers, fibres, waxes and tinsels has become a series of greedy rages for mere acquisition, but because fly-tying has been and still is a form of structured, digital dreaming. In the manipulation of fur and feather I recreate myself elsewhere, and while doing so, allow myself to become the fisherman I have always wanted to be. I did much the same with alcohol during the drinking days: whatever else I was doing when I was heedlessly pouring that ancient poison down my throat, I was – with the assistance of Dr. Vodka – posing. Confronted now with the fly-tying bench, I can and do tie up half a dozen Mallard and Blues under the shadow of the spire of Usquert church and I'm already halfway to Donegal and a big run of sea-trout. Tie up a handful of Raymonds and I'm already leaving for the bitter weather on the Orkney coast. Construct two or three Dubbel Dekkers and I'm sitting in the belly-boat on the wind-stricken expanses of a shallow limestone Irish lough, watching a giant streamer wave its underwater way past the dying lily pads where equally giant pike lie in wait.

Whip in the soft marabou at the tail of a Grå Frede and I'm three-quarters of the way down the shingles of a Danish beach with the stones crunching under my felt soles, watching the tide's edge for the movement of sea-trout to shrimps.

Fly-tying, like alcohol, also has its escapist side. That is, I crave sometimes to outwit, to outrun, to dodge the incessant pressures of work and other people. After the baleful engineering of another twelve- or fourteen-hour day (and the past year has been too full of them) then a position in front of the vice seems … safe. It's somewhere I know how to be; it's something I know how to do. For all the clumsiness and the occasional false starts, I'm both finally responsible and finally in control.

There is a difference, though, in these forms of addiction. The one, alcohol, will not only kill me quickly but will oblige me to end my days in introverted squalors and shame. The other, fly-tying, is much more beneficent, and its beckonings of imaginative recreation also have a practical and extraverted dimension for which I'm profoundly grateful. Fly-tying is also, mercifully, slightly cheaper than drinking a bottle of vodka a day – an activity which left me only with the perilous illusion of control and with only the fantasies of responsibility.

At its worst, of course fly-tying is an addiction, even a mania; but done gently it's a form of recreation whose end is the water's edge. I doubt very much whether fly-tying would land me in gaol, a hospital ward or a coffin, though I'm quite certain that alcohol would, sooner rather than later, ensure that one or more of those destinations would be my fate.

Still… Twenty-six fly-boxes. They range from oversize Dutch cigar boxes, in which I keep sea-trout tandems and Snakes or larger pike streamers, to plastic pill-boxes whose compartments hold dry flies whose hackles would be crushed in clips or foam. Poppers … Mayflies … Streamers for bass … Daddy long-legs … Gold-heads and grayling bugs… Traditional sea-trout patterns ... Salmon doubles ... Tube flies (including patterns tied from hair extensions) ... Two wallets full of pike streamers ... Stillwater buzzers ... Sedges...

How much of this radical abundance do I actually use?

I once fished part of a season in the north of England with just two flies, a John Storey and a Pheasant Tail nymph. It's true that I allowed myself to tie these two flies in different sizes (and in the case of the PTN, weights), but I caught just as many trout with those two flies as I would have done with twenty – or two hundred. That sounds enviably efficient, and in truth, it was. The problem, however, was that such fly-fishing among such self-imposed limitations wasn't very interesting. Fish taking caenis? Fine, offer them a diminutive (size 20 or even 22) John Storey. Trout on August Duns? Offer them a size 12. October grayling on needle-flies? Try them with a size 18 – though fish it in the surface film. Trout tailing on shrimps in a chalkstream glide? Catch them on a heavily wired PTN. Sedges at twilight? Size 10 John Storey tied bushy, and twitch it. Minnows? PTN on a size 8 longshank, nickel-plated hook ...

The constraints under which I was fishing gave me a healthy respect for the importance of presentation (rather than 'imitation'), but to be rigorously honest I also began to acquire rather less respect for the trout and all their indiscriminate greeds than I would have done by trying to catch them with better representations of what I thought they were eating. And therefore, after this very minor experiment had become somewhat monotonous, I returned to happy variety. The result was as if a Puritan had rediscovered music, chocolate and sex. I cast a fly thereafter with a smile on my face and a cheerful little fishing song in what was left of my heart. Angling apostasy helped me to love not only the sheer numbers of fly-patterns but also the endless variety of the techniques with which they could be fished. I sank – perhaps I rose – into mania, became multiple, experimental and profligate.

Fly-tying may be a mania, but it's a mania in which the technical, the practical and the aesthetic meet. Twenty-six fly-boxes? Wherever they began, and wherever they may end, then unlike other forms of mania and addiction, they have made me more than happy. With them and with the fly-rods I've travelled, even to places I've never been, and with that, always, I have been content.

11

29th December 2008
Christmas on the beach

Owing to an unforeseen change of plans I spent Christmas in an England which seemed somehow – though it's almost upsetting to use these adjectives – cheap, broke and dirty. The most casual flick through the television schedules suggested that the previous decades of greed and credit had somehow transmuted into the repeated, ugly self-exposures of game shows and the tired portrayals of fictional and celebrity unhappiness. Even those staples of English character, tea and irony, seemed weary and defensive. Almost everyone looked worn out.

The presumption of the television programme makers seemed to be that the entire population would spend Christmas day opening presents, then drinking, then drinking some more while the meal was being readied, then having some nibbles out of a packet, then drinking some more to take away the taste of the sprouts, then unsteadily toasting the Queen, and then just as unsteadily, and equally insincerely, subsiding in the direction of an unappreciated port and a sofa studded with lard, failed comedy from the 1970s, and shrink-wrapped, rum-dribbled mince pies.

Fortunately there is an alternative England. I find it each year at the Game Fair. I found it again early on Christmas morning, on Scarborough's North Bay.

It was bitter cold. A wan sun had risen from the North Sea, hesitantly lifted into thin tissues of cloud and shone uncertainly behind the silhouette of Scarborough Castle. The sea, murmurous at low tide and in a light easterly, sucked distantly at sand. On the rocks lying exposed at low water towards the north end of the bay stood nine cormorants, some drying their wings. Reared upright in the lambent ice of the nine o'clock light they looked like swastikas.

There were dogs everywhere. Behind them, in front of them, among them were the dog-walkers. They were men and women of a certain age – my age or older. Some carried throw-sticks; others carried binoculars; still others wore rucksacks in which, no doubt, were secreted the complete works of anyone not a celebrity chef, a map of the Trans-Pennine footpath, a copy of *Birds at Bempton: Gannets I Have Loved* by an anonymous author (Thwing Press, 1904), some shit-bags (one hopes, for dog detritus) and a flask of soup.

The dogs were having a splendid time. Clean, damp sand must feel wonderful under a dog's paws. Even the arthritic old-timers were running, or at least shifting a bit (and however arhythmically), along the beach. Occasionally, and in the way of dogs everywhere, greetings were exchanged as wet noses queried anuses. Ammoniac messages in the sand were sniffed as routinely as you or I inspect emails ... and then off the dogs would go, running again for no reason except for the joy of running. I imagined that inside every dog's head there was some canine exclamation mark which simply symbolised happiness.

If the dogs made me happy – dogs almost always do – then the dog-walkers first intrigued me and finally, cheered me. Apparently as far from the hangover as they were from the nonsense on the television, they had something to look after, something to do and somewhere to go, even if it was just to the end of the bay and back. Each manifested the kind of care which isn't measured by the indulgence of a worryingly expensive present but in time and responsibility. That is, the very fact of their dog-walking seemed in principle to be outwardly directed. Inland, in all the terrible lounges of England lounged overdrafts, ethanol and introversion. There on the beach, all of us somehow were, or had become, sane, wind-cheeked and extraverted. We met each others' eyes and said Hello. Shockingly, I fear we may even have smiled at each other. Well, why not? It was a cold Christmas morning; we were alive – though not quite as alive as the dogs; and we were outside.

The beach slowly emptied as the sun rose towards noon in low-slanted rays of light behind the closed guest-houses on the scarp above the North Bay. Seen from below, ivory- or off-white-fronted, they looked like a row of broken piano keys. On the rocks at the end of the beach the swastikas had been joined by other swastikas. If there's a collective noun for cormorants, it must be a rally.

Car doors slammed against the rally of cormorants. Tailgates were shut. The dogs were driven away from all the free parking spaces on the Marine Drive. The light easterly continued to blow. Grains of fine dry sand, and a strand of green tinsel, whispered across winter tarmac.

For an hour, it was the England I remembered. Call it the alternative England, or (suitably capitalised) the Other England. Perhaps, after all, it is merely the after-image of a middle-aged expatriate's England, as little to be trusted as those brittle and yellowing clichés about leather on willow, warm beer, pony clubs, vicarage teas and Miss Marple. And yet... Yet the reality was there to see on Scarborough beach, where somehow a few dozen English people met each other for the first time again, if only momentarily, and exchanged however brief a greeting while the east wind sniped at low tide and the dogs ran heedlessly on the sands.

Just before I climbed into the hire car I turned for a last look at the light on the North Bay. A hundred yards away from me and at the sea's edge stood a man bundled up in a down jacket against the cold. He'd raised a pair of binoculars and was urgently scanning eastwards into the distances of the North Sea. I followed his looking and squinted at the miles with naked eyes. Bird? Tanker? I saw nothing except the grey fastidious meeting of sea and sky. Then I looked again at the man. He seemed to be peering not at something there, nor at something coming closer and arriving. His posture, together with the intensity and duration of his looking, suggested that he was following something that was slowly disappearing, minute by minute dwindling, merging at last into the east, the cold and the weather and then vanishing into the horizon, where England somewhere was becoming snow.

12

5th January 2009
Pike, ice, and walking over fish

The Netherlands – all the Low Countries, in fact – have been frozen into something approaching paralysis. If it moves at all, traffic crawls at 40kph on mist-shrouded beams along motorways whose surfaces have become ice marbles. Ancient worthies in fleeces talk knowingly of National Skating Championships, even of a rare *elfstedentocht* (a skating marathon which slides through eleven towns in Friesland), while men in Fair Isle sweaters plumb the depth and density of the ice. Today, that depth has reached 11 centimeters (against a critical skatable depth of 12) and, with night temperatures of minus 13 expected, the freeze is set to continue while Holland sharpens its blades and the garden birds starve with cold, however I run after them with nuts and kettles.

Already we've lost nearly three weeks' pike fishing and we'll probably lose at least two more before the season ends. Yet, when the thaw comes, the pike often make up in numbers, and in the sheer intensity of the fishing, for the zero periods of the freeze. Perhaps that's why pike fishing has the reputation of being a largely winter pastime: long periods of cold, when the pike's metabolism is slow, are interspersed with short periods of relatively active hunting, often in the afternoon and at last light. Later January, and then the whole of February, are some of my own best times for pike fishing, judged on the statistics

for the past eight years, and they're particularly good for the fly rods, since at this time the pike quest again into the shallows – a minor and pre-spawning migration – and can be reached with intermediate lines, often at short range.

Caught here at the desk and frustrated at losing precious fishing time, I began to reconsider the whole business of the pike's metabolism with respect to ambient cold, and particularly, to surface ice. Author after author stresses that in the depths of winter the 'pike's metabolism' is slow – but why should that be? And what is 'the metabolism', anyway?

I thought back to the answer supplied to me and to Ad Swier by the biologist Marco Kraal as we worked on Ad's *Passion for Pike* (2006). In Marco's view, the pike's 'metabolism' can best be viewed as a set of chemical reactions fuelled by glucose. The operation of glucose is catalysed by enzymes, whose working is determined both by the pH factor of the water and (in particular) by temperature. In very general terms, when the water temperature increases, so enzyme activity increases (and with it, metabolism). As water temperatures decrease, so does enzyme activity (and with it, metabolism). There are also upper and lower boundaries to the optimally efficient working of enzymes, the upper boundary lying around 20°C and the lower boundary at around 5°C – at which last temperature, the molecules which are water begin to bind with each other, and the water therefore to freeze (Marco Kraal, in Ad Swier's *Passion for Pike*, 2006, p.127). It follows that at ice-low temperatures the pike's metabolism is relatively unstimulated by enzymes, and that at these periods the pike's appetite will be minimal or even altogether absent.

Marco's observations also help me to make sense of other fish behaviours. Sea-trout, for example, may on some southern Swedish rivers such as the Em and the Mörrum enter freshwater in the autumn and remain there until the following spring. Their metabolisms, too, are at a winter low; they don't eat while resident in freshwater – although they eat voraciously if and when they begin their return journey to the sea. (UK fishers often think of salmon (kelts) as behaving similarly.) And the charr in Greenland... I thought back to the thousands of sea-run charr I'd seen migrating upstream in September 2004 in the freshwater systems around Kangerlussuaq and Nuuk. What happens to them, once winter strikes? They lie, all but torpid, under the ice, until the spring thaw. When the thaw comes, those charr, like the Swedish sea-trout and like our own pike, too, are ravenous.

Those notes also help to explain the quality of pike fishing here in the Netherlands once the skaters have put their sweat-stained Fair Isle-pattern sweaters and fleeces back into the wash. I find that quality in later January and February in shallow waters – waters whose surface temperatures can warm quickly through 5 and then into 6 or 7 degrees. Sunshine can help. I don't mean that I like to fly-fish for pike when the sun is splitting the reeds – I do not – but at the end of a sunny day I've often noticed that pike will sometimes hunt avidly in the last hour of light. Measurements taken then with a water thermometer strongly suggest that the water temperature which has risen through that day to a short-term high of 6 or 7°C, just before darkness drops again and the surface water cools.

There are those anglers for whom these observations are 'too scientific'. I disagree: being outside, and trying to interpret not only 'what's there' but also how what's there, stays there, together with how it works the way it does, is for me as for thousands of others a matter of identifying *patterns*. The patterns are no less intricate, nor are they less beautiful, for being identified. Quite the reverse, in fact. The same suspicions of arid scientism also arise among graduates and undergraduates if and when I ever attempt to explain how the language of, say, a given poem works (that is, forms into patterns). Perhaps these people think that it's somehow irreligious to analyse anything, or perhaps believe that analysis is equivalent to vivisection. Yet as the great critic and philologist Leo Spitzer once said, unanswerably, when confronted by the the same brand of baleful scepticism: 'Great love prospers with understanding'.

While the surface waters of the Netherlands thicken into 12cm of ice I think of them out there, those millions of fish under the ice sheets. The roach in tight, almost motionless shoals; the perch in stationary groups; the flickers of momentary ice-light which are sticklebacks ... and the pike, still lying singly, tucked under the woodwork of a harbour walkway, or massively static in the casing of a conduit adjacent to a canal lock. It's like calling to mind a picture which might be engraved – an intricate, stylised dance – on an 18th century vase: *the sarabande of the fish*. Like me, they're waiting, though I wait with my impatient speculations and scraps of statistic while they wait, yellow-eyed, fin-nibbed, merely out of what we call instinct. Yet what is instinct but the chemistry of different hungers?

As I write, the sun is setting in an almost metallic yellow on the spire of Usquert church. The winter light is absurdly clear. In a moment I'll pull on three layers against the cold and walk with the Labrador down the smooth scree of evening sunlight spilling along the canal. Both of us in our different ways will be walking over fish towards the thaw – whenever the thaw shall come.

13

14th January 2009
Wings across the moon

I've never been particularly good at geese. One sort of goose has often looked very like another and until the last few years I would have been hard put to distinguish a Barnacle from a Brent, a Bean from a Greylag. The problem of identification was intensified when I tried to distinguish species from among

the various juveniles. Eight years ago, however, I set my own small fishing boat onto the waters of Vinkeveen, just south of Amsterdam, and since these lakes are significant overwintering grounds for geese migrating from the Arctic, I got to know geese a little better. I sometimes had the idea that in April and May I would see certain geese leaving for the high north, only to see those same birds come back in later October and November – great clamouring V-formations wheeling in over the Zuidplas while I set the boat for another slow drift across the drop-offs and dying beds of pondweed where the pike were about their autumn business. That is, I did not go to find the geese; the geese found me.

Some of the geese at Vinkeveen were Canada geese – an imported species – though there were undoubtedly some Greylags among them. The Canada geese were resident. Why, after all, would they make the long journey to Iceland with their relatives? There is food enough, in the form of plant growth, in and around the waters of Vinkeveen, and so these exiled geese are (or have become) resident, domestic. One of the bird books (*The Complete Book of British Birds*, eds. Michael Cady and Rob Hume, 1988, p.100) tells me that Canada geese are regarded by some among the birdwatching community with the same disdain others reserve for the idea of all-inclusive package holidays. That is, they're both 'alien' and common – common in the sense of vulgar, the avian equivalent of people living in Barratt homes (which last have always struck me, in contrast, as warm, easy to run and rather comfortable).

I did not despise them, those Canada geese Along with the wigeon, the geese were the voices of winter, and of loneliness. In the Wilnis polder south of Vinkeveen, for instance, I was accompanied all day by the bell-like honks of skeins of geese – they looked like detached strings of aerial muscle trying conclusions with the wind and cloud – while wigeon whistled throatily on rain-glazed or ice-freaked fields. Often enough I'd be the only soul out there in the boat, or trudging across the semi-frozen lands while the reed-plumes at the water's edge stiffened in frost. As the temperatures shrank below zero, the world looked so brittle I thought it might crack. Often, too, apart from my own steam-breath or the crazy race of a hare disturbed by the sound of approaching boots, the geese would be the only things moving in that gelid landscape of willows, far church spires and cloud-held distances.

Since we moved eighteen months ago to the Hogeland I've missed Vinkeveen, and the polders around it, but the Wadden Sea lies only fifteen minutes' bike ride from the tap of these hands at the keyboard. The Wadden (universally known as 'het Wad' in this part of the Netherlands) is one of the most important overwintering grounds of geese in Europe, and is home to many other species of coastal, estuarine and marsh bird. It's not difficult to see why: the Wadden, lying between the offshore islands and the coast, is shallow, to the extent that at almost every low tide vast areas of mudflats are exposed. For any birds migrating from the north – or for that matter, feeding their way up from the south – these mudflats must represent food, rest, and relative security.

The information boards at Noordpolderzijl tell visitors a great deal about *rotganzen* (Brent geese) of which 110,000 overwinter in the Wadden (www.waddenzee.nl), while Barnacle geese – 160,000 of them – make the long journey from Nova Zembla, although as with Canada geese and Greylags, many Barnacles have become resident: at the last count there were 7000 breeding pairs in the Netherlands.

One environment which all the geese find to their liking in winter is in Dutch called the *kwelder*. *Kwelder* is an almost untranslatable topographical term: 'marsh' is too unspecific and perhaps the closest word English has for *kwelder* is 'saltings' – that area of tundra-like land, often riven with muddy gullies, which borders the shallow sea. There are shellfish in the mud; there are salt-tolerant grasses growing from mud; and there is more mud, pocked with the siphons of razor clams. This also is the country of the redshank and curlew. For, or perhaps because of, its austerity, and certainly because of the open, salt-silvered quality of its light, I find such landscapes almost impossibly beautiful.

Two days ago we walked out from the harbour at Noorpolderzijl into the *kwelder*. The ground was almost entirely frozen and what under normal winter circumstances would have been a gloopy journey of boggy footsteps could be accomplished in trainers. A low sun struck at the land and five hundred metres to the north the sea sucked slowly at the edge of a tundra. There, resting near reed beds or drifting in the dirty, just-thawed floes which grated along the dock wall, were groups of geese, including what I'm almost certain were three White-fronted juveniles with vivid orange legs.

We walked back across the tundra as the light closed down. That night, while I lay still wakeful I heard the church clock strike midnight and then, high up, like a remote echo of a time before anyone had ever thought of naming the *kwelder*, perhaps even a time before the *kwelder* was, came the call of geese – ancient, fussy, urgent. From the warmth where I hugged myself I imagined that big V of birds riding the air, the slow, hoarse beat of their wings crossing the moon and the Pleiades, and thought of them descending just two miles to the north – descending, settling, gabbing quietly to each other that after navigating through magnetism, through storm, ice and isobars they had finally reached a habitation in the heart of winter.

I suppose that these days there are many who would never notice, many who would find geese and their winter journeys irrelevant at best. After all, it took me long enough to come round to noticing. I don't think the call of wild geese in winter would have meant very much to me for most of my adult life. But now, having become aware of the strangeness of the familiar, the noticing is like a rhythm. The days are punctuated by the appearance or the sounds of those natural things that mark time passing. Two nights ago, hearing the geese call over the house at midnight, time passed in wing beats, and I was so profoundly reassured that I don't remember falling asleep.

14

23rd January 2009
Of the Luce, or Pike

These have been dark days. An ice-bound Holland was recently replaced by a Holland stricken with torrential rains. While continual traffic sluices by on dipped beams at noon, the ditches are running thick with mud. Already we've lost six weeks of the pike season because of the freeze; the incessant winds and deluges now means that pike in rain-thickened water are more likely to take a static deadbait than even the most luridly coloured, slow-moving artificial lure.

There has of late been a bare half-day's opportunity to use the pike fly rod, and although the polders were still semi-frozen it was possible to cast here and there into patches of open canal. At this time of year and under these circumstances, then if one can find pike sheltering in at least relatively shallow water it's possible, sometimes, to get them to take a slowly fished streamer.

And so it was. After I'd moved what I'm sure was the same fish twice, I rested the lie for an hour, then came back to it from the opposite bank. There was no sudden, visible take. The line merely tightened in pewter water, and a few moments later a pike of around 6lbs made a surface swirl the size of a dinner table between the reed beds, startling the coots.

From nowhere, as I was drawing the fish to hand, the word 'luce' came to mind. *Luce* is of course an old name for the pike: Walton, writing in 1653, headed one of his chapters 'Observations of the Luce or Pike'. As I unhooked the big single from the pike's jaw I began to wonder about the etymology of 'luce' – and at the same time began to wonder just why pike

are called 'pike', and jacks, 'jacks'. The wondering, as always, drove me back to the *Oxford English Dictionary* (OED).

Luce, a term apparently adapted from Old French, which reproduced late Latin *lucius*, has been around from the 14th century, being first attested in some legal rolls from 1338. Chaucer knew the word: 'Many a breem and many a luce in stew' (*General Prologue* to the *Canterbury Tales*, 1386; Chaucer was clearly referring to the efforts being made in the later 14th century to keep pike in fish ponds (stews)). Late Latin *lucius*, the term adopted by Linnaeus in 1758 when he published his great system of classification, is odd, because the root of Latin *lucius* is *luc-*, related to *lux* 'light' and I've been unable to determine how, or even if, the Latin tag for the pike refers even indirectly to 'light'. (It may be that *lucius* is also related to the wolf, hence the byname for the pike, 'water-wolf'.) Interestingly, the latest attestation given by the OED for the word *luce* comes from 1892. That's significant, because since *luce* generally refers to adult pike, by the end of the 19th century the term *pike* (for the adult fish) had come into general use when contrasted with *jack*, meaning 'small pike'. I also find it significant, even useful, that the OED has not yet marked *luce* as obsolete.

The word *jack* is again relatively old, dating in general use as a proper name (*Jack*, probably from French *Jacques*, and a byname for *John*) from the 14th century. By the late 16th century the term *jack* has come to have a meaning specific to pike, as the following interesting quote, from 1587, attests: 'The pike as he ageth receiueth diuerse names, as from a frie to a gilthead, from a gilthead to a pod, from a pod to a jacke, from a jacke to a pickerell, from a pickerell to a pike...'

For many centuries, therefore, it would have been possible to refer to young pike either as *pickerel* or as *jack(s)*, though the implication of the 1587 quote is that a *jacke* is smaller than a *pickerel*. *Pickerel* is attested in English in the 14th century, being comprised of *pic(k)* – with the addition of the suffix *–el(le)*, which last was borrowed from French and has the semantic effect of diminishing or trivialising the sense of the root, cf. *bagatelle*, *demoiselle*. Once the term *pickerel* is exported to North America, however, probably in the 18th century, the lexical range of *jack* seems to spread within the British Isles, to the extent that some later writers use *jack* to refer both to young (male) pike and to the adult fish…

It's a lexically crowded history. There were once, after all, two words for adult pike – *luce* and *pike* – and (at least) two words for 'smaller pike' – *pickerel* and *jack*. Perhaps because it's a native word (dating in its sense of 'pointed thing' from at least the 8th century and Old English *pīc*), and is so sheerly descriptive of the predatory spear-point that is the pike's head, the word *pike* wins lexical ground over *luce*, while *pickerel*, safely exported elsewhere, gives ground to *jack*.

There was a further word to throw into the lexical brew I was concocting, and that is the Lowland Scots word *ged*. I wondered whether the word was somehow exported to Lowland Scotland from Scandinavia at the time of the Viking settlements in northern Northumbria and elsewhere (Old Norse *gaddr*, 'spike', present-day Danish *gedde*) but it seems more likely that the word survives in Lowland Scots as a survival of Gaelic *geadais*.

I looked at the photograph I'd taken of the pike I'd caught on the streamer the day before. An eye looked flatly back at me, looking neither wolvish nor malicious but rather, looking merely surprised. The head of the fish, though, was indeed pointed, clean-lined, predatory. Seen from above, a pike's head – particularly, the head of a big pike – does look somewhat like a blade of some kind, and it doesn't seem accidental that the genius of several different languages has invented vernacular names which alike relate to spears, points and spikes.

Etymology, however, is a bad guide to angling, and I prefer not to attribute deliberate malice to the pike, whose nature is neither as violent nor as disastrous or wilful as the human spears and points from which it was named. I don't like anthropomorphism in fishing, even when it comes as an apparently inevitable part of the lexicon embedded in the hobby, and so I suspect that from this point on, given the choice 'of the Luce, or Pike', I'll prefer the *luce*.

15

27th January 2009
Counting the holes

The first fly-reel I owned was an Intrepid Rimfly, bought in 1968 for something like 2.10s.6d. The reel could be converted from right- to left-hand wind by the strong tweaking of two triangles of plastic which lay on the inner face of the drum, held there by something which looked and felt like a sprung-metal hair-clip. The metal was painted what might kindly be called gunmetal grey – a grey which was subject to chipping, blebbing and flaking. It was the piscatorial equivalent of scabies. No wonder the reel's ratchet protested: it was, literally, a scream, although a sousing in raindrops would mean that the scream subdued to a mute, loose chattering – the rattle of granny's teeth.

I loved that reel. With it, and with the much-dressed, much-abused level silk line bonded to it, I caught my first trout; first sea-trout; first grayling. I used the reel on northern English becks; in saltwater; for the mayfly; for mackerel. The reel was in continual service from 1968 until 1979, when, feeling disloyal, I bought a secondhand Beaulite which was then to the Intrepid Rimfly as a Bentley was to a Citroën 2CV – though the comparison with the 2CV does the Rimfly a disservice: it was much more reliable than a 2CV, and it was also faster, cheaper, and utterly British … to the extent that it would never nip off for a quick Gauloise, nor indulge in a Gallic shrug. No: the Rimfly was, always and everywhere, a thing of Capstan, tea and sandwiches; of Sunday afternoon tinned red salmon. Very possibly, the Rimfly was made from the same tins. I don't care. The Rimfly was magnificent.

I last used the reel at Driffield in 2007. Thirty-nine seasons on, having endured at least half a dozen changes of government, three continents, twenty-three different fly-lines and far too many fish to count, it was almost as good as new. Almost. In truth, the Rimfly has lasted nearly as long as I have, and it's therefore co-extensive with all the crankiness and imperfections that are … well, that are me. Having once been as well-engineered as time and circumstance could have made us, both of us have developed over the years a certain amount of tolerance, to the extent that we've begun to evince a creak here and there, a wince, a telling stiffness; the odd, inexplicable rattle; a worn-out play between the body and its peripheries. It doesn't seem to be accidental that we've both become, in our own ways, minor memorialists. If we're lucky, we shall both eventually be framed; if not, the dust shall claim us and we shall be utterly forgotten.

I write in homage, but I'm also writing out of curiosity and frustration. For the past seven weeks, for instance – yes, it's seven weeks now – I've scarcely been able to fish. Holland has been frozen, and its good burghers have been gleefully sharpening their skates. For the fly-fisherman, the advent of outdoor ice-rinks and lurid lycra betokens nothing more than long sessions at the fly-tying bench and a continuously administered dose of tackle-tinkering. As part of the tackle-tinkering, naturally I greased and slicked, buffed and sorted, polished and palavered; I wiped down, made good, had a good whip the while, and among the whiles, oiled what parts of the fly-reels and wheels need to be oiled.

I did not count how many fly-reels and spools I possess. It's not that I would be embarrassed to tell you; I would be embarrassed to tell myself. Instead, I fingered some of the best parts of my own history, in the form of the Intrepid Rimfly, and because I couldn't go back to Then, nor fish in the Now, I began to count the holes.

There's no crying need for a fly-reel to have holes cut into the drum or spool. I suppose the holes are so cut for three reasons: (i) they allow the reel and line to drain; (ii) they save weight; (iii) they look nice. If I speak for myself, I rather like to see the fluorescence of the backing, and then the colour of the fly-line, neatly arranged there under the portholes of the spool. And therefore, from practicality, from the physics of rod-weight and line-speed, and from aesthetics, the holes are cut.

There are, for the record, 34 holes cut into the spool of the

Intrepid Rimfly, standard 3½-inch model. Based on original prices, that works out at 1.485 shillings a hole (equivalent to 17d. in the old, decorative currency or something like 7p. in today's logic).

I fingered a few more fly-reels: makes from Hardy, from Greys, from Partridge; old Loop graphite reels, new Loop CLWs; Loop Evotec G3; old and new System 2 reels… And then, at last, I picked up a recent acquisition, a secondhand Danielsson and spool which are so beautifully engineered that I can barely bring myself to leave fingerprints on the ultra-smooth, refined scurf the space-age cutting machines have left on the metal. The two together – reel and spool – cost something like 200 Euros.

I counted more holes. There were very many to count. Again for the record, five large non-circular holes are cut in the drum, and 70 holes (large and small, circular and oval) cut in each spool: 75 holes, therefore. At the secondhand price I willingly, even covetously paid, that works out at 0.26 Euros a hole.

Calculated purely by the hole:cost ratio (HCR) and on today's exchange rates, then the Danielsson costs 24p a hole – just over three times more expensive than the Rimfly, though no adjustment has been made here for cost-of-living increases between 1968 and 2009, and I suspect that in 1968 an Intrepid Rimfly cost, in real terms, the best part of a day's wages – which would make it dearer, comparatively speaking, than the Danielsson.

'Uh? Counting the holes? The HCR?' you query. I can hear the incredulity, and know that you'll shrug – you'll possibly shrug Gallically – and then turn away with a dismissive 'Get a life, Chris' dying on your lips.

Ah, but I had a life, a rich life, and many parts of that rich life have been enriched by the memories I hold in my hands every time I pick up a fly-reel and try the play between drum and spool under my fingers, listen to the smoothness of the check, or pull away a yard of line against the brake. And where did those memories begin?

They began with learning how not to tie an arbour knot; with sealing the end of a level silk line at the edge of a match flame; and then reeling the backing, the silk, the lot onto an Intrepid Rimfly.

16

1st February 2009
Nights of the Pink Pig

Since the beginning of December last, there have been a mere three days when the waters of the local canals and polders have been free of ice. I've fished precisely twice – that is, I've fished exactly twice, rather than fished twice and done so with precision. Precision has been impossible in these mostly sub-zero temperatures. On rare ventures to the banks I've been bundled in down. Casting streamers at winter-torpid pike, I've looked like an overgrown chicken hurling smaller chickens among the remains of ice floes.

The polders are frozen again. The courtyard is freaked with snow – not benign, noise-muffling snow but a sort of shrill, gritty white left there by overnight blizzards. 'I'm just going outside,' I say to no one as I fumble again into three layers of winter gear and grope for the dog's lead. 'I may be some time.' Each evening, back in the frail tent of the study, I've retreated into work, into fishing dreams and fly-tying. I've tied more flies over the past two months than at any other period of this angling life.

One pattern which has entranced me, and entranced me because it's moderately tricky to tie, is the Pattegrisen. This is in essence an Öland Shrimp adapted to attractive life among Danish saltwater sea-trout. Tied on a size 4-6 iron, and utilising long, trailing strands of salmon-pink marabou or swept-back Spey hackle, the thing is colloquially known as the Pink Pig. Sitting there in the vice, all sprightliness, filminess, with feelers in the form of stripped white hackle stalks, with shrimp-eyes attached, it looks wonderful ... to me, at least. Whether the fish will like it is anyone's guess, although since there's no fly which will *not* take a saltwater sea-trout (so the cliché runs on the coasts of Fyn), then I expect it will work. On a normally myopic evening bent over the vice I can reasonably expect to complete three such Pink Pigs. Outside in the darkness, ice storms dunt at clouds, and clouds mar stars. I look out through the skylight windows and watch the luminous dial on the face of the clock on Usquert's church spire fracture into snow and become obscure. I turn back to the vice, and Nights of the Pink Pig.

If I allow myself to wonder where this intricate absorption with saltwater sea-trout began then I can date the moment precisely: April 1st 1995. In 1994 I had read somewhere about the angling and environmental project the Danes were undertaking on the island of Funen (Fyn), and had brazenly invited myself on an angling visit with a view to constructing a brace of feature articles about the project for *Trout and Salmon*. The kind response to my letters was a suggestion that I should travel in early April. I confess that for all my reading and even some of my experience, I thought that was odd: schooled on sea-trout in the west of Scotland and Ireland, I associated these fish largely with the summer and early autumn. To fish for them in April was, I thought then, merely … strange. After all, April was the month one associated with Large Dark Olives, brown trout in rivers, or with buzzers on stillwaters… But … sea-trout? In the sea? In April?

I knew no better, then – although I should have done. I smile at myself now.

On that first 1995 trip I was met and was hosted with very great tolerance. After I'd landed in Esbjerg and driven the short distance to the island, everything seemed to happen in fast-forward. I was whisked off towards meetings with the project leaders and coordinators; I was told what the programme of my visit would be; I was between-whiles instructed, gently, about the ways of coastal sea-trout; I was waltzed away towards dinner… But before the waltzing, the meeting and the whisking I was told, again gently, that I had to do some fishing.

I looked out at a cold April evening. It was already 6 o'clock, and a chill wind blew from the east. My contact, Steffen Hinchely, waded into the waters of the Gamborg Fjord carrying a space-age 7-weight to which was attached a small, greyish shrimp pattern. I stumbled after him in plastic waders, carrying an old reservoir rod and a venerably stiff intermediate line which at some point in its life had decided that sinking was too much trouble and that therefore it would partially and randomly float.

Steffen kept wading, casting between steps. Seen from a

distance his technique looked like the performance of a top sportsman or artist: all ease and elegance. His truncated silhouette dwindled into the watery distance. A hundred yards shorewards, still in the shallows, I lengthened line and cast – if it could be called a cast – towards a horizon which was rapidly becoming sheathed in bitter darkness. The whole process felt bizarre.

I cast the shrimp towards what patches of deepening mauve could still be discerned on the bottom. The mauve represented patches of seaweed. Elsewhere, extended splodges of British Racing Green indicated underwater eel-grass beds. I was still fishing in water that was no more than knee-deep. Certainly, I thought, it might just be possible to move a fish which had come into the shallows at dusk ... But that would be in summer, surely? I mean, this – I squinted into pewter light, with the whole fjord stretching to right and left – this just can't possibly ...

The venerable intermediate pulled away into the semi-dark. The fish hooked itself. Ten yards away I caught a glimpse of a silvered flank. It looked like a streak of crystal under the clear green surface. It was hard to work out which of the two of us, angler or fish, was the more surprised. A moment later and I'd played the fish to hand, supported it briefly, and slipped out the hook. It was a beautiful spring sea-trout of around 2lbs, a living muscle. And that, within twenty minutes of first arriving on the shores of the Gamborg Fjord. Astonishing.

Over the past fourteen years I've continued to be astonished on Fyn, though the astonishment has deepened into a slower and more understanding enchantment. I've never found the fishing easy, but the island has occasionally yielded some good catches as well as what is to date my biggest ever sea-trout, a fish of 8½lb. which hammered a streamer late one evening in early October.

I'm proud of very little, and certainly I'm proud of almost

nothing in my fishing. Nevertheless, some years ago, ten years on from 1995, I stood with Steffen in late March outside the walls of the new hatchery in Odense. We were waiting to go out with the batches of smolts which were about to be stocked into some of the becks which feed the Odense Fjord. It was again bitterly cold. Steffen was smiling. 'You were one of my first, you know,' he said. I didn't understand. 'You were one of the first writers ever to come here and tell the story of the Fyn project, back then in 1995.' He paused. I didn't know quite what to say. There was a short silence in which Steffen looked at the foot-wide transparent pipes through which were rushing tonnes of sea-trout smolts. 'Now just look what we started.'

I started nothing, of course. All I ever did was lend the Fyn project a pen. Yet many years ago, feeling clumsy, cold and utterly foolish, I waded out with Steffen Hinchely into the Gamborg Fjord late on the evening of April 1st, and caught a sea-trout. Something changed, at that moment; something in life slipped into a new alignment. It's that alignment to which I return, in hope and memory, on these Nights of the Pink Pig, where somewhere else in time a man is stupefied by fish and darkness and then wades into the sea.

17

9th February 2009
On subtlety (Part One)

It's often a small thing which can trigger angling speculation and along with speculation, memory. What has prompted these words, for example, was no more (and no less) than the construction of some Silver Doctors, size 8. They weren't 'authentic' Silver Doctors, either – those patterns specified in Courtney Williams' great *Dictionary of Trout Flies* (5th edition, 1973) as having wings comprising red, yellow and green-dyed swan or goose feather-slips sheathed in or (better) topped by fibres of mallard (p. 305). I used dyed bucktail instead of swan – green over red over yellow – a fact which I suspect will make little difference to the sea-trout, but which yielded a wonderfully translucent effect when the flies were held up against an electric light. The bulb shone through colours: where the bucktail held against the ribbed silver of the flies' bodies there was sparkle, even brilliance.

They knew a great deal, those fly-tiers from fifty, even a hundred years ago. Last April, for example, browsing in Malone (*Irish Trout and Salmon Flies*, 1998), I stumbled on a west-of-Ireland sea-trout pattern, one first noted in 1886 by 'Hi-Regan' (John J. Dunne): the Torc-Lan. I tied it: orange and black seal's fur substitute; a brace of hackles (black followed by blood red); a turn or two of blue jay at the throat; folded bronze mallard... Again, flies of colour, brilliance, and translucency were the result, although as with the Silver Doctors, the light-scattering beauty of the patterns was only revealed in transmitted light. That is, the patterns looked at their best as they would be seen as the fish, looking upwards, or sideways-and-upwards, would see them. In clear water, such patterns are easily, temptingly visible, and it seems no accident that Hamish Stuart, fishing at the turn of the century before last, recorded great success among the sea-trout of Hebridean *machair* lochs using the Silver Doctor, while I'm certain that the Torc-Lan will be highly effective in some clearer west-of-Ireland sea-trout systems. I think of those in north Mayo and parts of Donegal, for instance, rather than the peatier waters of Connemara, where blacks and clarets, silhouettes rather than translucencies, reign supreme.

An evening after I'd made the Silver Doctors I found myself

replicating some patterns for Danish sea-trout. I'd come across the dressings in the electronic pages of a Dutch fly-fishing internet site. They were dressings which represented stylised shrimps – all trailing white marabou, a few strands of flash, and a big … head? thorax? … formed from several turns of pillar-box-red chenille. The patterns were easy to tie and resulted in vivid blocks of contrast. I'm quite sure they'll be wonderful attractor patterns for sea-trout hunting in saltwater along the Danish beaches but they were by no means as technically challenging, nor as translucent, as the Silver Doctors I'd tied the evening before.

I therefore found myself reflecting, on a long train journey during which I was supposed to be working, on fashion in sunk flies in general and on delicacy and translucency in particular. It seems to me, as I begin to consider today's much-favoured stillwater and sea-trout patterns, that we may be beginning to lose the ancient insight of designing and tying our artificial patterns in the ways we conceive *the fish* might see them. Instead, we tie flies which are labour-extensive and cost-effective; eyecatching (to us); and which rely on contrast and high-impact visibility rather than on the brilliance of mixed natural fibres and/or on translucency. Perhaps – I thought to myself as a frozen Drenthe slid past the train windows in freaks of frost – perhaps we're in danger of forgetting subtlety.

I pondered further. That wonderful old nymph, the Pheasant Tail – yes, it is old, now – is often replaced by something tied with silk under the herls and a gold-head: quick to construct, but lacking in the relative translucency of the original, where pheasant tail fibre is lapped over very fine copper wire. Stillwater fishers desperate to catch trout by almost any means have invented Blobs. Grayling fly-fishers have discovered (and often seem to rediscover) the fatal allure of imitation salmon eggs, patterns which are no more than twists of fluorescent yarn on a hook. Salmon fishers have largely abandoned the brilliance and translucency of married wings for bucktail fibres whipped onto tubes or Waddingtons, or more recently, onto coneheads. Tubes, Waddingtons and coneheads: the design of the terminal gear, admirably, even mercilessly utilitarian, to some extent duplicates, and maybe even exceeds, what was possible in the old dispensations of artistry – a well muscled delicacy, a strategic angling tact – with rod and line. What we knot onto the end of our leaders, these days, is often the fly-fishing equivalent of fast food.

On the one hand, I admire the incessant inventiveness, the technocratic energy, of today's enviably skilled fly-dressers. I realise that I have tied and used many hundreds of the 'fast food' patterns, and also know that no angling lure has ever been invented because it makes the catching of fish less efficient. On the other hand, I wonder, very gently, whether something has been lost as time hurtles on mechanical wings into the future: finesse; an ability to intrigue and convince with natural fibres; a reciprocity with materials.

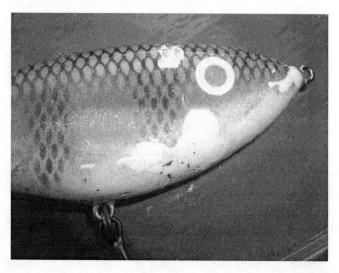

Strangely, perhaps, I find the same lack of subtlety in some forms of pike fishing. Take jerkbaits – and yes, I can hear you scoff at the analogy, since very few anglers associate jerkbaits with 'subtlety'. Still, I do associate the two, largely because my own most successful jerkbait, a lure which has taken around a dozen fish of between 100 and 110cm, and has also taken one leviathan of 118cm, is an unobtrusively coloured, much-repaired Robbait 7 inches long and weighing a mere 70g. It's become battered and tooth-marked, yet I know quite well that if I fish it correctly – that is, slowly, enticingly, *artfully* – it has the potential to pull any pike that swims. By contrast, many of today's jerkbaits, and their fashionable American after-comers, the pullbaits, can measure up to 14 inches long and may weigh upwards of 150g. Such lures would I suppose be difficult to cast; they're designed merely to tow behind a boat all day. Nevertheless, I suspect that very soon the first purpose-built 'pullbait rods' will be marketed, rods capable of casting lures up to 200g. Bigger, faster, more efficient – certainly. But better?

Matters seem to be similar with pike streamers. Far and away my own most successful patterns are 7-inch-long Flash Flies, tied in copper, silver and green(ish) Flashabou, therefore highly reflective *and* translucent, which I've made by the dozen and find easy to cast and handle. Elsewhere, however, I've heard pike fly-fishermen brag about the sheer size of their streamers, exhume one from a wallet the size of a coffin and display something the size of a gosling which is a miracle of rabbit strip, glitter, rattles, fluorescence, mock raccoon and glue. As the thing is reverentially passed from hand to hand one can almost hear gasps of awe.

I'm not here pleading for 'imitation', nor for some form of 'purism'. I'm simply recording what seems to be today's obsessions with efficiency, technology and results, at the same time wondering aloud whether (and if so, to what extent) we might have lost, or be in danger of losing, the pleasures of subtlety in angling.

Is subtlety pleasurable? Last night, soon after the last of three coats of varnish had dried on the heads of those Silver Doctors, I unclipped them from the foam, selected what seemed to be the best of them and held it again to the light. Red, yellow, green; a glitter of reflections and tones; a sheen composed of seething westerly cloud-bright on a Donegal estuary where the sea-trout are moving...

18

10th February 2009
On subtlety (Part Two)

...Red, yellow, green; a glitter of reflections and tones; a sheen composed of seething westerly cloud-bright on a Donegal estuary where the sea-trout are moving...

And of course, as I lurch among angling memories and turn them into angling hope, I'm also puzzled by myself. In terms of subtlety, for example, I very greatly admire the old-timers and their manipulation of natural feathers and fibres but at the same time I'm radically attracted by today's utilitarianism and its democracies of invention. Part of me is Puritanical, a stern proponent of the pared-down, the simplified and uncluttered. Another part of me is the Cavalier celebrant of the Gothic, the extravagant, the historically legitimised beckonings of ornateness. What a muddle I have brought into middle age. The most I can hope is that I will never insist on any single part of the muddle, and it does seem that we are surrounded, even in our fishing and fly-tying, by a culture of insistence in which everyone is looking for a guru, and in which each would-be guru is prepared to insist. That way, angling cults are born. The stench of burning martyr is sniffed on the breeze of the evening rise; the ever-nearer sounds of the witch hunt disturb one's concentration on the *thwock* of a sea-trout moving at twilight under the shadow of the far bank.

Pity.

I don't dispute and am happy to acknowledge that there are those fly-dressers – they're more skilled than I'll ever be – who are adept, even expert in the antique. Last year, I was invited, by what was no more than a kind mistake, to take part as a fly-dresser in the Dutch Fly Fair. There were I suppose around sixty of us, from three different continents. We sat at long trestle tables in an outbuilding and the great angling public drifted in twos and threes, – sometimes, in the case of famous tiers, in knots and clusters – past our workplaces. Of the sixty tiers, more than fifty seemed to me to be specialising in the construction of ultra-large pike streamers, the sort of creations which elicited muted squeaks of astonishment from spectators. Another nine tiers specialised in the creation of traditional salmon flies – those gorgeous irons decorated with married wings of twinned red, green and blue swan, or tied Irish-style, with an underwing formed from golden pheasant tippets. As the wings were married, as the silks were lapped, there were more muted squeaks, as well there might have been. The results could have been, and perhaps were, framed. Nevertheless, it interested me that what were being demonstrated were largely *techniques*. No one seemed to ask whether the pike lures or those beautiful salmon flies would actually catch fish and if so, why they did, although it seemed to me that lightness of dressing, translucency and colour were the absolute keys to the former success of these old salmon patterns. Held to the light, as the married fibres now held and now transmitted brightness, such patterns shimmered with the illusion of life.

A day or two later and I went back to the pages of Malone. Many of the oldfashioned sea-trout patterns listed there use translucency as a key constructive principle: either the bodies are composed of mixed seal's fur or the wings are layered out of tippets, swan fibres and bronze mallard – or both. Dozens of the trout patterns, too, particularly those of the sedges and hatching mayflies, incorporate a touch of translucency, and I was intrigued to see how many of the flies which one would use at twilight and beyond incorporate some hint of orange in their makeup. In other words, the gorgeousness and abundance of the flies wasn't there to be merely *admired*; it was there because that very gorgeousness increased the attractiveness of the fly *as the fish would see it* in different conditions of overhead or underwater light. The flies, that is, were demonstrations of tactical subtlety rather than tokens of the tier's self-display.

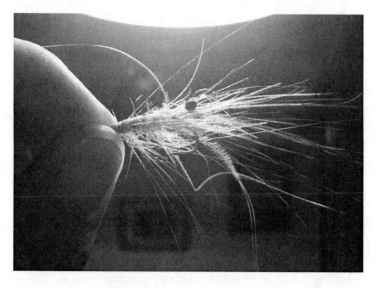

I learned much from the Dutch Fly Fair. For the record, I sat there with a portable brass vice and a shoebox half full of materials feeling like a fraud and a fool. Instead of tying pike streamers (for which I hadn't brought the components) or traditional salmon flies (for which I didn't have the skills) I sat and tied Funneldun, those supremely effective upwinged representations designed in the 1980s by Neil Patterson. After I'd completed several hours' solitary work a couple of anglers stood in front of my tying-space. 'I hope they don't ask questions,' I thought, nervously. They asked questions. One of them even pulled out a pocket computer and asked if he could take notes. 'I'd be delighted,' I mumbled. 'Oh yes,' said the visitor. 'We can tie some of these at our club's winter fly-tying evenings...' I sat there silently whipping, embarrassed at feeling pleased. A few moments later and a tackle dealer from the north-east of England stood by the desk. 'Don't suppose you can tie up any caenis patterns?' he asked. He fished some of the great Northumberland stillwaters, and had been troubled by late-evening hatches of the Angler's Curse. As it happened, I knew those waters, and also had some size 18 and 20 up-eyed hooks with me. I improvised a dozen caenis patterns – minute things with hollow fibres for tails and with translucent bodies – and thought no more about it.

A month later I was at the UK Game Fair, walking down a sweltering Fisherman's Row. A massive hand was clapped suddenly to my back. 'Chris,' boomed a voice. 'Those caenis patterns...' There was a pause. Were the patterns no good? Had they fallen apart? *McCully, Royaume Unis ... Nul points?* 'Those caenis patterns were bloody wonderful. Don't suppose you can tie up some more for us, can you?'

Since then, I've tried to return to subtlety, not simply because it's satisfying but because it seems to work. This past winter, for example, alongside the technocratic primary colours of the usual pike streamers I've dressed Flash Flies with mobile mixed wings which are highly translucent; I've begun to experiment with mixed bucktail wings under bronze mallard for certain sea-trout patterns, including the Silver Doctor; and I've discovered, belatedly, some the the intricate, translucent and mobile shrimp patterns some Danish fly-dressers and anglers have developed for coastal sea-trout. It pleases me that some of these last patterns, including the famous Öland Shrimp (Pink Pig), have their ultimate origins in the generic shrimp-fly designs intended to be fished over salmon fifty or even a hundred years ago.

Finally in this context, I know that if I've brought muddle into middle age then the muddle spreads across both angling and writing. If I'm caught between the Puritanical and the Cavalier in angling then it's the same with words, and particularly, with verse. In terms of verse writing I'm greatly attracted to the spare, the pared-down, the resolutely non-metrical and demotic, but at the same time I'm pulled towards the tuneful, the polyphonic – an impressionism of sound. A couple of years ago, while translating Old English poetry each morning and completing a sequence of classically themed original poems each afternoon – activities which left me feeling almost schizophrenic – I looked out wearily at the winter darkness one evening and sighed to no one that after all, in terms of mastering the many and various verse writing techniques, one simply had to be able to 'do everything'.

In angling, thank goodness, I'll never be able to do everything, yet I've found, and keep rediscovering, that subtlety is no bad place to begin doing whatever it is one wants to do.

19

19th February 2009
Pike under Venus rising

After nine weeks of frost, the waters in this part of the Netherlands became free of ice last Tuesday. Even the *slootjes* – the ditches – have thawed. Although we haven't yet heard the song of the first blackbird of spring, the snowdrops have appeared, and now and then there's a pitiful and chaotic twittering from the hedge where bluetits couple in a whirr of protest and static wing beats. Late snow still disfigures the hellebores, but the ground is very slowly softening. In this hinterland which is neither winter nor yet spring, and just before the end of the pike season, again it's time – high time – to think again about trying to catch a pike.

Yesterday I looked up after a morning's work and decided that squinting through proofs and double-checking copyright permissions would be a baleful way of spending the afternoon. I shrugged into jacket and boots, put a flask of coffee into a shoulderbag, picked up the 9-weight and set off for the northern polder, where the pike just might possibly be sidling into the shallows. Every year I've noticed this localised migration, from the deeps where the pike spend the bitter weather of January back to the dead reed stems and vegetation in the shallows where, in a month or so, the pike will spawn. Accordingly, in any relatively ice-free winter I've had some wonderful pike fishing with the fly rods in later January and throughout February – a fact which baffles many UK-based friends, who associate February's snow flurries with the compulsory arcana of dead-baiting. Further, fishing the fly properly involves presenting it in relative terms more slowly and searchingly than would be possible with many a moving lure fished on a multiplier or fixed-spool reel.

It's not easy. The problem, always, is finding the pike. As February progresses the fish begin to lie together in twos or threes. Many hundreds of metres of water can be devoid of pike, while fifty metres further up you may have a dozen follows or takes from small, pre-spawning groups of fish. The groups usually comprise one or two males (jacks), plus one larger female. The earliest I've watched pike spawn here in the Netherlands was March 3rd – last year, in the mildest winter for decades. The latest I've seen them begin spawning was March 26th.

There was a cloudy sun, a cool breeze from the south which veered uncertainly towards the westering light. I covered water by sluices, dead reeds, sullen drop-offs – water which had yielded a bare handful of pike over the past months. Nothing happened except the squall of huge flocks of geese on the skyline by the sea dyke. Occasionally I changed the 4/0 Flash Fly for a 6/0 Red-head Bunny Bug. Nothing went on happening, and then a bit more of the same nothing happened which had been the same nothing a few moments earlier. If I looked up into the afternoon the light was so open and the sky so vast that I began to sense the curve of the earth at the horizon. I felt that I was casting the streamer under a huge inverted bowl of air and cloud.

At a junction of two small canals a grey-green shape slid from a near-bank reed bed and annexed the Flash Fly. A few moments later and a jack lay in the reed stems at my feet, was unhooked – a twist of the hand to free the streamer – and swirled back to its lie. A small fish, granted, but it focused attention. Perhaps it would be lying near a bigger female. I covered the water more diligently, with better concentration, varying the speed of the retrieve, allowing the lure to sink and flutter, to hang there, then to speed upwards, then to hang again. The lovely thing was that in such relatively clear water I could sight the streamer at the end of the retrieve. It still surprises me, how often during the course of a session there's a spear-shaped head, a pair of predatory eyes, following the lure. And then the hurtle of a flank as a pike turns on the prey…

Fifty metres towards the sea from where I'd returned the first pike I moved another. This one had followed the streamer from mid-canal, and finally nipped at the lure six paces from my boots. I failed to hook it. On the next cast the pike came again, a swift flash at the lure as flaring tinsels neared the bank. It missed its target. I cast once more, intent. This time, the pike made no mistake, the hook fastened, and a minute later a small fish of 5lbs came to my outstretched hand. Like many pike here in the clay polders of the north-east, this one had a beautiful silvery sheen to its pristine scales. Three leeches fastened to its belly testified to its recent period of near-coma under the ice.

It was instructive, that little pike, reminding me that in a cold February the pike are still at least relatively torpid. They rarely hunt all day and it's often just the warmest hour of the afternoon in which they choose to hunt. (If that hour coincides with dusk, so much the better.) They may also take three or four goes, on consecutive casts, to annexe a moving lure. The angler's job then is to respond appropriately to each moving pike and above all, to give the pike time to get its shot in. In late winter, a pike hunting a moving lure is a pike driven by radical pre-spawn hunger. Once moved from its torpor, such a pike can usually be caught. Indeed, it's not at all uncommon, at this time of year, to catch the same pike twice.

I fished on and within ten minutes moved another fish. This one loomed after the streamer in mid-canal, disappeared, reappeared, and then took in a flare of gills close to my feet. No pike, this one: a flash of mottled brown, striped flanks in silver. It was a zander, of around the same size as the pike I'd just returned. I still have no idea how it shed the hook.

I moved no other fish. It was past teatime and the cold was falling in as the light darkened. You could feel the tension of winter leak back in the air. The low sun was veiled in cloud and would soon extinguish itself on the rim of the world.

Before turning homeward I stood for a moment and looked westerly at a landscape turning back to monochrome. There in the faint remaining blue of the sky was Venus rising. It's the brightest object in the westerly evening sky at this time of year – so bright and so apparently large that on some evenings I try and fail to see the contours of the planet's surface.

Associated for millennia with cosmic imagos of womanhood – Venus has been known as Ishtar, Aphrodite and Hesperus (a word that's related to the more familiar 'vespers') – the planet rode there in the west, a symbol of day sliding into night, yet also the day-bringer, April's morning star. Its steady, unnaturally bright light hung over all the polders stretching west through Friesland; over copses, nubs of towers, knots of villages; over the geese gathering in thousands on the mudflats and *kwelders*; over the veneer of ice reforming at that moment on the muddy green lees of ditches.

I turned finally for home, asking myself what these slight encounters had meant. I couldn't tell. I could tell only what they'd included: an uncertain, middle-aged man; two small pike, intent on prey, hunting into the sun's extinction – and then Venus rising, a visible vesper at the lip of the certain dark.

20

25th February 2009
Recaptures

How many of the fish we catch have been caught – more or less recently – before? The number is probably much greater than we think. At this time of year, for example, it's almost commonplace to catch the same pike twice, sometimes within minutes and from the same lie.

The first time I was certain that I'd secured a recapture was on a raw February day on the Wilnis polder south of Amsterdam. The fishing waters consisted of small pools an acre or two in extent which collected into narrow, eastward-running channels. These waters were nowhere more than five feet deep and the channels were very shallow indeed. Nevertheless, as January turned into February the pike would slowly quest into, and then lie in, the channels, sometimes in a mere foot or two of water. There, in what were no more than ditches with attitude, the pike would eventually spawn.

It was wonderfully exciting fishing. The channels were

waters which would interest a small boy with a minnow-net, let alone a middle-aged man with an 8-weight fly rod. There, in shallows carrying a clear brown stain from the underlying fen, there lay pike into double figures. To watch the swirls and bow-waves of such fish as they accelerated explosively onto the streamer in a foot of water was something almost heart-stopping. Then the rod thudding over ... A whorl of water the size of a dinner table ... The great moment where a cold, wet hand is slipped securely under a flaring gill-plate ...

Before I got to know the fishing at Wilnis well, I used to explore the pools and channels with a spinning rod and a smallish tandem spinner. An unweighted Mepps Tandem Maximum, in white or fluorescent green, was the lure of choice in these early piking days. I habitually nipped down the barbs on the treble and then set off for a session carrying no more than a pair of unhooking pliers, a tape measure and a flask of coffee in a shoulder bag.

On the February day in question – blue-black clouds scudding across the lower sky and a wind with north in it – I hooked a small pike in one of the channels, close under my own bank. As I lifted out the fish, briefly admired it and then slipped out the treble I noticed some deep scars along the fish's right flank. So symmetrical were the scars, and so deep, that at first I thought the pike had been damaged by dredging or cutting machinery, but no such machinery had been at work that year in the polder. Nor did the wounds look like the result of a heron-stab. As I was safely returning the fish I concluded that the half-healed wounds must have been made by those baleful pests of inland waters, cormorants.

Because pike often lie together or in small groups in the very early spring, I immediately covered the same ground again with the same lure. I had a second take, in exactly the same place. I played the pike to hand, slipped fingers under its gill plate, and ... It was the fish I'd just returned. There could be no question, since I was staring at the same pattern of half-healed wounds on the fish's flank.

I would very much have liked to have had this minor angling incident televised. After all, if that little pike had been so terrified, so traumatised, so hurt by the fact of its initial capture, *would it have subsequently taken the same lure, fished in the same way and at the same speed, in exactly the same place, within a minute of being returned the first time?*

I was relatively inexperienced in terms of pike fishing, back then. I ascribed the incident to a fluke and wrestled with my conscience while I completed the fishing diary that night. Did I record that I'd caught one pike, twice? Or that I'd caught two pike, both being the same fish? As it was, I settled for the first option, but held the memory of the recapture somewhere in the dim set of preoccupations and half-connections which comprise my angling brain.

A year later, this time fishing a tiny (size 2) streamer on the fly rod in the same set of channels at the same time of year, I had a repeat experience with a pike of around 6lbs – a fish instantly recognisable since it lacked a pectoral fin. A year later, and again in February (though on a different polder), I caught another pike on the same spoon – a Kuusamo Professor – on three consecutive Saturdays before the season closed. That last pike, however, wasn't as significant, in terms of whatever it may or may not have felt during its capture, as those pike which seize a given lure within minutes of being hooked, landed and returned after taking exactly the same lure.

Three days ago, fishing in Drenthe with the fly rod, I caught a pike of 80cm on a Flash Fly (4/0). It was a particularly strong pike and it was securely landed and returned. I covered the same mark again three hours later – and caught the same pike on a 6/0 Red-head Bunny Bug. Later, I moved to a tiny canal I'd never fished before. The big Bunny Bug moved a pike immediately: a massive displacement under the streamer, and then a slack line. The pike came again on the next cast, and this time it took the lure – an accelerating lash of power. I felt a brief pressure on the rod and then, somehow, the hook came away as the waves subsided. I left the fish to itself for five minutes and then returned to it. A large, half-submerged pipe ran into the end of the canal. I more than suspected that the pike would have retreated to the shelter of the pipe end and would be lying there with its body inside the pipe and its primeval head at the pipe's edge. At the same time I was thinking back to the recaptures of the season, and of all the seasons. Although this pike had taken the lure a mere five minutes before and been hooked, albeit briefly, in the process, then I felt that it wouldn't be reluctant to take the same lure five minutes later. I drew the streamer across the mouth of the sunken pipe, and…

It was 83cm, that fish, and the second – or was it the third? – double-figure pike that day. I was delighted.

It's significant, perhaps, that these incidents seem to take place most readily in February, when the pike are collecting in the shallows and where they hunt and feed intensively if they hunt and feed at all. Nevertheless, the recaptures suggest that when a pike is hooked and returned it does not feel 'pain' as humans can ever understand it. They are not 'traumatised' by the shocks of capture – how could they be, when they take the same lure again within minutes? – nor does the fear they must indeed experience during the moments of the play seem to translate into an unwillingness to hunt again almost as soon as they're returned to their proper element. Further, and last: like all other fish, pike have no scale of comparison since they have no reasoning powers with which to make comparisons; they can't think, for example, 'the fear I experience on being hooked is greater than the fear I experience when I sense the shadow of a cow grazing at the water's edge pass over me'. Whatever fear they feel cannot be relativised, since evolution wouldn't have been so cruel, nor so profligate, as to equip creatures such as fish with relativising powers. No: here as elsewhere, nature's simply red in tooth and scar, and these pike recaptures may well reveal how red.

21

6th March 2009
Bird song

The months between early December and mid-February are unusually silent. You get up in the dark and come home in the dark, and rarely in either dark does a bird sing. If you hear bird noise at all it is likely to be those voices of winter, the robin or the wren (which last is appropriately called *winterkoning* – 'winter-king' – in Dutch). Occasionally, on an evening in later January, the freaked song of the mistle thrush attempts and fails to codify itself against the wind. Out in the polder, too, there are the throat-whistles of wigeon and the cries of the high geese. But from the true songsters there is no sound. The resident birds are voiceless; the summer migrants haven't yet arrived.

At some point in early February and possibly, in an unusually mild year, late January, there comes a moment when spring seems to blink awake in the middle of winter. It's a calm evening after rain; wet still glazes the rooftops. Dark falls in over the parks, the playgrounds, the urban canals, and as dark spreads, there on a perch atop the gable of a house there are the first tentative notes of the blackbird's spring song. On the first day of song you might hear only one or two blackbirds. It's as if they're trying their throats for tunefulness. The next evening, however, if the weather remains at least relatively still, there will be dozens of birds singing, and among the blackbirds'song there will also be the songs of the thrushes.

This is one of the great moments of the year, and every year, from as early as mid-January, we listen for the first blackbird of spring. Each year, too, it has been Monika who has heard the first notes. February 7th … February 13th … In 2008, after the mildest winter in Dutch meteorological history, it was January 23rd, and a blackbird singing its heart out from a perch in a tree just outside Groningen railway station.

This year, however, I heard the first blackbirds in the half-light of dawn on Tueday, 24th February. They began to sing late in the month, possibly because we've had such a severe winter. But there their voices were, on a still, damp morning I'd had to struggle blearily into along with some equally bleary old clothes. As I led the dog out onto the road for her morning walk I paused. From just behind Claas's house came the first notes, mellow and unmistakable. I looked at my watch: 0647. During the following quarter of an hour it was as if bird voices had somehow benignly infected the air: sound swam from perch to perch, rooftop to rooftop, tree to tree. For an instant, it was spring. I walked home smiling. Even the dog was smiling.

At these times I often think of Edward Thomas's wonderful poem 'Adlestrop'. His train, you'll recall, has stopped unexpectedly at a station – Adlestrop – in late June. The protagonist of the poem looks out through the window of the train, and what he sees are trees and the rail-side grasses, fragments of June cloud. At this instant of his seeing, a blackbird sings ... and a more distant blackbird – and another, more distant still, until their combined singing spreads from the train window and its momentary epiphany of sight and sound, away past what the eye can encompass, and embraces all of Oxfordshire and Gloucestershire (Edward Thomas, 'Adlestrop'. In ed. R.S. Thomas, *Selected Poems of Edward Thomas*. London: Faber and Faber (1964), p.48). From that unasked-for blink of apprehension spreads not only bird song, but counties, local geographies, England.

Why do birds sing? The usual answer aligns bird song with mating and with the desire of males to claim and defend territory. It's probably the fittest birds, the birds most apt to be selected for mating, which sing, while song-dearth – lack of, or slowness in repetition of song – in individuals may indicate the presence of parasites or disease. Bird song, then, is very often a sex strategy, the occupation of a space which proclaims 'I'm here, fit and available. Choose me.'

That helps to explain, of course, why it is that resident birds begin to sing in very early spring. First, sufficient food is a precondition of song: an adult songbird is after all announcing his fitness. Second, the development of the eggs needs to take place in optimal temperatures, and once hatched, the young birds need enough time, during the summer and early autumn, for sustained feeding so that they have the best chance to maintain themselves during the following winter (and to reproduce the following spring). There would be little point

91

in birds rearing young in the autumn: even if the eggs were to hatch, the young birds would subsequently starve. Bird song therefore brings with it the instinctive sense of appropriate temporal alignment found everywhere in the natural world. Many fly-fishermen encounter something similar among runs of young sea-trout, which migrate to saltwater in late April or May. This arrangement allows them the maximal opportunity to find food on the coasts and in the estuaries before many of them return to freshwater as herling in the later summer.

On the other hand, there is a small amount of bird song in autumn, and this can't be explained by the imperative throats of natural selection. In *The Charm of Birds* (1927), Grey of Falloden, describing the autumn songs of the starling, argued that 'Some birds may sing from nothing but a sense of wellbeing when they are in good health, and not depressed by moulting or adverse weather' (p.125).

The day after I'd heard the first blackbirds I took the fly rod and went out late in the afternoon to the northern polder to try for a pike. The canal, running due north, lies close to the sea, and its western bank forms the boundary to many acres of stubble. After an hour of fruitless exploration with the big streamers I stopped, took out the thermos, and sat on conveniently sloped earth alongside the canal. From away to the north, out on the *kwelder*, there were the long conversations of geese. Somewhere on the eastern bank the sky gathered into a moment of weeping: curlew. Fifty yards to the north-east, a blackbird liquefied a gable. The song began first as a series of uncertain, cello-like notes, but progressed into something assured. It was as if the slanting light itself had coalesced into a stream of sound. And then, westerly, unmistakable, from somewhere behind my head came the simmering, minute-long expectancies that could be nothing but skylarks.

At that instant, indistinguishable from the endless instants which had preceded it through the months of silence and darkness, winter became spring. The birds knew it; because they knew it, they sang it. I sat on the bank, a middle-aged man cupping a mugful, and listened, profoundly grateful, to voices becoming chronicles extending to local topographies. Sitting there in my own Adlestrop, I couldn't help thinking that beyond the clarity of need, the teleology of selection and the economy of time, the birds were singing out of a sense of profligate abundance which is also called joy.

22

18th March 2009
The distance between York and Zwolle

If the late 1960s were Sergeant Pepper and psychedelic chrome, the 1970s were purple, cadmium yellow, and flock brown wallpaper. Musically, it was glorious: Bowie was Ziggy, Roxy smoked Virginia Plain and Dylan was writing 'Blood on the Tracks'. While the rest of Europe was getting stoned and making red-bulbed lamps out of the hulls of wine bottles, for me the 1970s were the decade of the first sea-trout, the first hurting erection and the first kiss.

I didn't altogether prosper at school. The failure to prosper was nothing to do with the school and everything to do with the mess that was me. The days passed often enough in a kind of turgid boredom: the boredom became turgid during the endless adolescent moments of acute selfconsciousness. The selfconsciousness came from that perennial terror, an over-active ego. The ego had been a nice present from Sigmund Freud. Sigmund Freud came from God. And God lived in York, a short walk from Bootham Bar, at Bulmer's.

Bulmer's sold fishing tackle. It also sold red-bulbed lamps which had been made from the hulls of wine bottles; clothes pegs; stacks of secondhand magazines, including back issues of *Trout and Salmon*; kettles; horse brasses and ironing boards.

One of the good things about being schooled at Bootham was that its liberal and Quaker ethic transferred trust. During school mealtimes, for instance, pupils were trusted to walk the short distance into the city in order to have lunch. They were also trusted to come back to school again afterwards. I suppose the elders imagined that we would dine under the shadow of York Minster on tea, ethical buns, and lettuce which had been hand-crisped on the thighs of the unfortunate. As it was, while the clock ticked over to the stroke of one we would race out onto the brief island of lunchtime in the general direction of tooth-rotting sweets and, as a concession to healthy eating, chips from the local fish-and-chip shop. The chips were occasionally supplemented by scraps – crisp leavings of batter. 'Chips 'n' scraps, please.' We couldn't afford the fish that went with the fish 'n' chips, though occasionally we were flush enough to afford a polystyrene tub of baked beans.

After we'd eaten the chips we hurtled towards Bulmer's. In an hour-long lunchbreak there was just enough time to run from school to the chip shop (which was hard by The Shambles), and from there to Bulmer's (which lay ten minutes' worth of indigestion and stitch away in the opposite direction). The schedule allowed for a further ten minutes' of window-shopping. Very occasionally – perhaps once in any given school term – the window shopping became a sale. In spring 1972, for example, I bought a pile of back issues of *Trout and Salmon*. In autumn of that year I made a major purchase: a 12-foot Daiwa coarse rod which I was subsequently to use for at least twenty years and on which I was to catch grayling, rudd, perch, ruffe, gudgeon, roach, trout and even mullet.

I still have that rod. At some period in its illustrious history I must have re-ringed it, since the whippings are now a subdued and tidy dark red silk as opposed to the purple and cadmium yellow original tyings, but by today's standards the rod is a nonsense. It's as whippy and tippy as a hair. So hairy and soft is it, I venture that the rod isn't made out of fibreglass at all. I suspect Daiwa's rod-makers constructed it out of brown flock wallpaper. I suspect, too, that they were stoned at the time.

I hadn't thought about Bootham lunchtimes and Bulmer's for many years – until the past month. Each Monday, during these past few weeks of non-spring, I've travelled from Groningen to Zwolle in order to teach. Each Monday morning I've offered a how-to course on 'Writing a Scientific Article in English'; each Monday afternoon I've tried to teach the telephonists at Windesheim Corporate Academy – delightful ladies, all – something about saying 'Hello' in English. ('Hello' is always a winner, one finds.) Between the scientific article and the hours of Hello lies the island of lunchtime.

Zwolle, like York, is a medieval city and like York, it's sited in the heart of a very good coarse fishing area. It would be unusual, I thought, if Zwolle did not have some sort of fishing tackle shop. Because I thought, I checked. It did. 'Faunaland', which functions as a pet shop as well as a tackle shop, could be found, the map told me, a short lunchtime walk away from the classrooms in which I was otherwise engaged trying to earn part of a living.

One has those moments of *déja vu* in which one is mugged by strange likeness. Three weeks ago, as the indecorous and middle-aged sprint began which was to take me from the classroom to 'Faunaland', I was again mugged. The mugger was, of course, a culprit well-known to me. He was the boy who much more athletically had sprinted towards the chip shop and Bulmer's decades before.

'Faunaland' sells bird seed, dog leads, whistles, parrots, ice skates and hamsters. But the hamster part is only the front half of the shop. At the rear, there's an extensive annex which sells fishing tackle. Go in there and you have no choice but to sniff the arcane aromas issuing from bags of strawberry boilies. It's the piscatorial equivalent of getting stoned. While stoned, you can finger rods, rests and Rapalas. It's wonderful.

As it was, it took me two lunchtimes of virtual shopping before I plucked up the courage to buy anything. I settled on a spool of 40lb. test PowerPro.

Recent linguistic research suggests that native speakers of a given language can detect foreigners – those using that language as a second or other tongue – within 0.40 seconds of the foreigner opening his or her mouth. The chap behind the till at 'Faunaland' went one better. I proferred him the spool silently; I reached for my wallet, equally silently. 'Good stuff, PowerPro, isn't it?' he asked, in accentless and perfect English. He looked somewhat like Erasmus, too. Perhaps he was Erasmus, moonlighting among boilies, stealing time in tackle shops away from his editions of Jerome.

I paid, feeling self-conscious. The self-consciousness stemmed from an over-active ego which had been wrapped in brown flock wallpaper by Sigmund Freud. Sigmund Freud had been given to the world by a God sheathed in turgid clouds of cadmium yellow and purple. And all the spiders from Mars had migrated to the local chip shop.

It was, after all, a God-awful small affair. As I sprinted stiffly back to the Dutch classroom in which I was to teach the world to say Hello, I tried to work out the distance between York and Zwolle.

We don't live in literal geographies. The places from which we've travelled and to which we must return are all, always and only imaginative constructs. At the end of the constructs, as

Freud, Bowie and Erasmus in their different ways have tried to explain, lies merely what Yeats called the desolation of reality.

Give or take a term or two, the distance between York and Zwolle is thirty-seven years.

23

31st March 2009
Ragworms and the moon

It was a long way to go – a round trip of 1000 miles – in order to encounter a handful of small sea-trout and catch just two of them. Yet the journey to Fyn in Denmark has become an annually twice-repeated pilgrimage which I wouldn't miss for all the German roadworks and traffic queues in the world.

This spring, I was in search of ragworms. Somewhere adjacent to the thousandth set of traffic bollards cordoning off large parts of the motorway between Bremen and Hamburg, I reminded myself that the prime objective of the trip was if possible to catch a sea-trout which was feeding on ragworms. A secondary objective was … it sounds risible, put like this … a secondary objective was simply to *see* a ragworm. I started to laugh, there in the car as the traffic inched pointlessly forward in the direction of nowhere specific in North Rhine-Westphalia. *Middle Aged Yorkshireman Fails in Ragworm Hunt.* I haven't stopped smiling since.

Local Danish fishermen are very keen on catching sea-trout on ragworms during this early part of the spring. Apparently these crack anglers sidle into tackle shops and ask 'Har du orm?' – roughly translated, 'Got any worms, mate?' – in the sort of hushed, embarrassed tones usually reserved, these days, for buying cigarettes. The *ormer* having been duly obtained, they are threaded up size 2 hooks and offered to the fish on a sort of rolling paternoster. The fly-fishermen, however, to whom a paternoster is a sort of prayer (to be intoned after the three thousandth cast of the day has failed to move any sea-trout whatsoever) and not a sort of end-tackle, must be content with ragworm representations tied on tandem size 4 hooks whose shanks are liberally wrapped with black-green cactus chenille and varnished with a secret preparation called Hope Eternal.

I'd heard a great deal over the years about the ragworms of spring. Each year, come late March or early April, angling worm-rumours would reach me. *This German chap, now – he had five good fish down at Torø… And that German chap, well, he had a fish of 3.75 kilos down near Assens … Yup, ragworm.* For some reason, worm-rumour loves these German fellows. Apparently they, too, are escaping from roadworks, slipping into tackle shops all over North Rhine-Westphalia and hissing 'Hast du orm?' across unsuspecting drawersful of

Sherry Spinners tied for those difficult Austrian dusks on the summer-shrunk Traun.

Yes, I'd heard a great deal and I dare say much of it was justified. The ragworm, that is, is for the sea-trout angler a worm of spring. It's in spring, and reliably around the first full moon of March, when ragworms breed.

Peter Hayward's excellent *Seashore* (London: Collins New Naturalist Series (2004), pp.50-51) explains that ragworms, including the commonest species, *Hediste diversicolor*, live where they do in the silts and muds of intertidal zones found typically in estuaries and large sea bays because they're very tolerant of differing salinity. This is convenient for those sea-trout which overwinter in saltwater, since they will usually spend the cold months in areas which are at least brackish, having a low tolerance for high salinity during the winter. Often, therefore, the sea-trout will be found in exactly those places and conditions of low salinity tolerable by the ragworm. Further, explains Hayward, ragworms anticipate their own spawning by turning into a modified form called an *epitoke* – a word I had to look up ('the posterior sexual part of the body of certain … worms' OED). This epitoke – I was becoming entranced by the terminology – in order to swim develops enlarged and broadened parapodia… (*Parapodia*. More myopic muttering at the dictionary: 'rudimentary limbs'.) Once the limbs have been broadened and the creature can swim, spawning takes place at night, when both males and females gather in swarms at the surface of the estuarial shallows and shallow, silty bays, at which times eggs and sperm are shed with relentless abandon into the sea, after which the creatures die. It's a sort of saltwater worm-orgy, a glittering and miniature frenzy under the pewter light of a cloud-hindered moon.

I arrived on Fyn after an eight-hour drive. It was already dusk – a cold, wet, March dusk with a rain-filled south-easterly lashing at headlands. I debated silently whether to tuck up with a plate of cheese and biscuits and be sensible or whether to don the neoprenes. The donning won. I drove to a mark north of Risinge Hoved which I knew would provide the only piece of shelter on that part of Fyn's eastern coastline. I pulled on the neoprenes in the rain; tackled up in the rain; tied on a newly made tandem ragworm pattern in the rain ... and lurched down the beach (in the rain), where dusk was becoming dark. It was the first sea-trout trip of another season and like any 10-year-old, I simply couldn't wait to fish.

If it was madness, the insanity was filled with luck. I hadn't been casting for more than ten minutes when I spotted a moving fish not six yards from my wading boots. It was no more than a displacement of dark light among water and stones. But it was there. I cast the tandem (in the rain) just upwind of the movement. The sea-trout took, and was apparently well hooked ... until it wasn't. I cast again, and before you could say 'epitoke' I hooked another. This one, mercifully, came to hand – 13 inches or so of bright-silver, well-conditioned little sea-trout, the sort of fish the Danes call 'Greenlander'. Ten minutes after returning that one to the night and the gale, I hooked another.

It was a complete fluke, coming across these fish moving in knee-deep shallows on the last of the tide and light. In retrospect I'd have liked to have killed one of those little sea-trout in order to confirm that it had indeed been moving to rags – the fish in the shallows could, after all, have been hunting shrimp rather than our common-as-silt 'intertidal polychaete' – but since the size limit on the Danish coasts is 16 inches I obeyed both the letter and the spirit of the law, and went without a sea-trout breakfast.

The following evening I fished on until the last of the

light failed over a wind-washed sky and the Odense fjord..
It doesn't seem coincidental that the Odense fjord – a large,
shallow and sheltered area of water – offers good sea-trout
fishing in winter and early spring. It's an expanse whose
waters are both relatively warmer and more brackish that the
open seas outside the fjord entrance, and since the bottom
of the fjord is largely muddy, this is prime ragworm and
ragworm-breeding ground.

It was a couple of days after the new moon. I was wading
back to terra firma in a dim glimmer of light which allowed
me to make out the bottom as I waded. Bladderwrack;
horned wrack; stumps of mussel beds ... And there, writhing
by some tendrils of filamentous green and red weed, was
a ragworm. I suspect it was *Hediste diversicolor*, since it
was only around 15 centimetres long (whereas the king rag
can grow up to 50cm), but it was quite big enough to have
made a wonderful meal for a winter-hungry Greenlander. I
peered down as it writhed. I had a very good peer indeed, as
a matter of fact, bending in thick neoprenes until the seams
squeaked. The worm squirmed away as if coy. 'No need to
be shy,' I said aloud. 'They're only slightly enlarged and
broadened parapodia, after all. Could happen to anyone.
Nothing to be embarrassed about.' The worm disappeared
under a clump of weed.

I'd found my ragworm. I'd caught my sea-trout. Another
season was underway and, as I pointed the car south and west
again in the direction of all the traffic-stopping engineering
between Hamburg and Bremen, I was smiling.

I was grateful, you see. It may have been madness, but I
was glad that at last I could look those Danes and Germans
in the eye and talk *Hediste diversicolor* like a man.

24

2nd April 2009
Fools, fake swans and floatant

April 1st marks the traditional opening of the trout season. I'm well aware that these days many fly-fishers will have begun their angling year weeks or even months earlier, throwing 10-weights and big tubes over salmon and the expensive expanses of the Tay; poking about with 4-weights and dry flies on the Devon Barle; manipulating a DI6 sinker and a big lure over shoals of March rainbows. It's also true that in recent times I'm more likely to open my own trout season by fishing for sea-trout on the coast then I am to head for the upper reaches of the Wharfe and a hatch of Large Dark Olives. Nevertheless, April 1st – All Fools' Day – is a date resonant with all the Aprils and all the openings past, and I ungum my eyes on the morning of that date with something approaching relief. Whatever the weather forecasters may or may not say, winter is over. There's also the thought, if one has survived 50, that you've been spared for another spring, and all the loved, familiar things are before you.

There are relatively few times in the year when you have tacit permission from the gods to wave two polite fingers in the general direction of a world turned even madder than usual, but April 1st, a compulsory fishing day, is one of them. I almost ignored the ridiculous and incessant calls of work (I worked, impatiently and badly, during the morning), then waved – and went.

Baggelhuizen, lying in the north-east of the country near Assen, is an 11 acre pond stocked with rainbows by the *Noord Nederlands Vliegvis Vereniging* (NNVV – North Netherlands

Fly-fishing Club). Because, almost uniquely in this part of the country, it offers fly-fishing for rainbows I fish it on perhaps a handful of occasions each year. It's relatively quiet; it's not a 2-acre hole in the ground; and the fish, which average a touch over the pound, are generally in good condition. There are also good hatches of midges, hawthorns and sedges, so it's possible to fish the dry fly – not that I'm a dry fly fetishist (far from it). After pike fishing the winter through with big streamers, and after the shrimps and ragworms of the coast, it seems charmingly simple. It's also occasionally very exciting, to fish a dry fly over stillwater rainbows.

The afternoon brought a glitter of light and a cold NE breeze. When I bought my ticket at the club-house I was told that some few fish had been taken 'behind the fake swan' – a life-size wooden model which adorns (if that's the right word) the pond's western bay. I don't know why the Dutch have this remarkable enthusiasm for launching wooden replicas of birds and fish onto the surfaces of otherwise innocent sheets of water. On one estate lake I fished a few years ago, the owners had installed an alarming and lurid replica of Jaws. Perhaps it wasn't coincidental that I caught some rainbows of an almost equally alarming size, but all the same, I could have lived without the dayglo shark.

At Baggelhuizen I tackled up near the fake swan, keeping a weather-eye open for the nebs of rising fish. I had the pond to myself. A chaffinch sung its heart out from a bramble bush; a woodpecker was doing its stuff in a birch on the far bank. I thought of the words of Edward Grey: for the fly-fisher in April, he wrote, the air itself holds 'an appeal, a promise, a prophecy'. The season, and all its fake swans, lay ahead. Then I found I'd forgotten to bring any floatant.

From April to September you'll usually find a tin of Mucilin, a bottle of Permaflote and a dobber of Gink about my person. Because I'd been fishing on the Danish coasts last week, however, where at this time of year sunk flies of various kinds are *de rigeur*, I'd somehow overlooked the tin, the bottle and the dobber. Strange, because my fishing is very often a matter of obsession, double-checking and lists. Usually, little is forgotten. In the event, it didn't matter. I was carrying some hybrid Hopper and Hawthorn patterns which had plenty of CDC in their dressings – those wonderful, buoyant fibres which are key constituents of what a friend once called, unforgettably, 'Duck's Arse Flies'. They float without a stroke of Gink, particularly in a light ripple.

There was the odd fish showing. For long periods the surface would be merely a glitter of light, and then somewhere at a ripple-edge you'd spot the ring of a quietly rising fish. It was enough to keep me at the dry fly, though I suppose if I'd been sensible I'd have fished a sinking line and a big lure (Black Marabou, Tadpole, White Lure…) and caught a heedless half-dozen. As it was, I stuck with a dry fly which became increasingly and satisfyingly damp. It rode down in the film. I fished it static, with occasional soft twitches: a struggling insect.

Sporadic clouds formed and re-formed; a wren flitted about in coppiced willows under my back-cast; a spawning frog hopped away as I waded gingerly across shallows. I began to think about Aprils and openings past. I'd usually caught a fish or two each opening day and had seen the catch as a harbinger of things to come. To draw a blank there at Baggelhuizen would seem... But then again, wasn't it enough, simply to be there, enjoying the precise rhythms of casting and presentation? Simply to be outside? And how many trout does a man need to catch in one lifetime? Five thousand? Ten thousand? Would it matter if I blanked? Well, no (...but then again, maybe).

In the midst of maybes, I cast in the direction of the fake swan. It was four in the afternoon. The surface continued to glitter; I'd caught nothing; worryingly, I'd risen less. I felt foolish, persisting with the floating fly. Yet fish continued to show, very sporadically. 'Work it out, Chris.'

The wind was moving left to right along the north shore. At the western end was a small bay. Any surface-borne insects, I thought, would be pushed by wind and ripple towards this curve. Any underwater currents, too, would act similarly. Surely there'd be a fish nosing about in that western bay, perhaps working up the drop-off?

There was. Out of the corner of an eye I noticed the smallest of rises eight yards to my right, close in towards the bank. I cast back-handed, angling up the forward cast so that the fly would land softly. I could just make out its pin-head silhouette at the ripple's edge. Suddenly, quietly, the fly was annexed. That rainbow was a well-conditioned fish of 17½ inches and 2lbs 4oz. Ten minutes later, I got another – a fish which was so anxious to secure its meal that it rose three times on three consecutive casts.

I went home feeling pleased with myself. A brace of 2lb-ers, after all, is no bad way to begin a season. But what had pleased me was working out exactly how the fish would be

105

behaving. 'Yes,' I thought to myself, 'it's often the same with these buzzer-feeding fish. You can usually find them just off the ripple at the downwind edge of the breeze in some sheltered bay. Black midges ... Buzzers ... *Chironomus anthracinus* ... Buzzers...'

When I did the autopsies that evening, those rainbows turned out to be stuffed with large black beetles. There in the darkness at Baggelhuizen, a fake swan was stretching its wooden neck, then shaking its head in smiling disbelief.

25

12th April 2009
On not catching ide

A glance at Muus and Dalhstrom's *Guide to the Freshwater Fishes of Britain and Europe* (1971) indicates that the ide, *Leuciscus idus*, is a fish native to continental Europe. The western limit of its distribution runs south-west through Austria, west into Germany, and then north-west into the Netherlands. The fish doesn't appear to occur as native to the British Isles, although I have a dim memory of seeing another distribution map from another source which indicated that this migratory chub did indeed occur naturally in some freshwater systems in and around the Fens. More certainly, however, I've never seen any articles in the English angling press about fishing for wild ide, while Dutch angling literature contains many such references, particularly as these relate to catching ide (a) during their migratory probings into running water during March and April and (b) during their sojourn back in stillwater during the summer months. During both periods, ide can be caught on the fly rod.

Although the ide is on the Red List of protected and endangered species in the Netherlands, there are, here and there, some fairly good remaining stocks of these fish. In the provinces of Groningen and Drenthe, shoals of ide certainly occur in the Lauwersmeer, a former arm of the sea which is now a freshwater lake connected to the Wadden Sea by sluices, and it seems likely that it's these Lauwersmeer ide which make their upstream migration south-easterly through the Reitdiep and from there, many kilometers southwards again, into the Peizerdiep (see for example Brouwer et al. 2008, p. 64). The wanderings of the ide have been greatly assisted in recent years by the removal of obstacles in the watercourse such as dams and locks, which in some (though not all) cases have been replaced by stepped weirs up which the fish can run.

As March turns into April, many UK fly-fishers twitch and imagine casting olives over rivers filled with rising brown trout or buzzers over stillwater rainbows. In Groningen, the twitching, accompanied by small, unignorable beating on angling's bush telegraph, relates wholly to the ide. Are the fish making their migration yet? '*Jawel. Gisteren ving ik een paar mannetjes in de stuw...*' (Certainly. Yesterday I caught two small males just under the fish-trap...) It puzzled me at first, since the mentions of ide-catching were invariably gendered: *I caught males; the females hadn't arrived...* Then I went back to Muus and Dahlstrom and found that male ide arrive in the spawning places some few days before the females (p.96).

Together with an exceptionally skilled friend – one of the most terrifyingly able fly-casters I've ever met – I resolved, if only once, to try and catch a spring ide. I was encouraged by the fact that Rudy had caught three the week before during a dawn session. These were males to around 45cm. 'The females generally arrive later, during the third week of April,' he said, with utter confidence. He's clearly a giant among ide.

I got up in the dark. The morning, windless, smelled of spring – starlight on the taut globes of tulip petals, on the first-cut grass. Our tail lights sped redly through the lifting darkness, southwards into Drenthe. By the time we reached the weir there was already the first smear of light along the eatern sky. We tackled up with 4- and 5-weights, and tied barbless, beaded nymphs which looked for all the world like Red Tags in costume jewellery onto 4lb. points. 'The touch of red helps,' said Rudy. 'Maybe it stimulates the ide's aggression. Fish it like a little streamer, in small strips.'

It's rare in the Netherlands for any angler to fish by the sound of running water. The weir was three-tiered. Below the lowest tier the water acquired a sort of baritone rumble to accompany the sussurations of the top tier and the alto sighs of the middle one. Fifty yards below the current I cast downstream, below the baritone rumble, and fished the costume Red Tag back in small strips, as instructed, while the fly-line swung round to the right. In that semi-dark I was reminded incongruously of sea-trout fishing. On every cast I was expecting the pull of a taking fish. None came. I worked downstream, away from the baritone rumble and towards a bed of first-growing lilies swaying there like ladies' skirts in some lovely underwater orchestra.

Rudy called across from the far bank. 'Did you see that?' I'd seen nothing. Then I looked more closely, and saw the after-ebb of ripples. An ide had moved close in to my bank, within six inches of the stones. I covered it – of course I covered it – but felt nothing that cast nor on subsequent casts. Just occasionally there was a swirl, a ruck of water as an ide went about its spawning dance, but according to Rudy it wasn't amounting to much: 'If the males are here it's a real commotion'.

I stopped after a while. Rudy went on casting, an exquisite stylist. As the light came up I began to discern the loop of his fly-line against a stain of cloud at the bottom of the sky. I sat under a hazel and opened the flask. There was the smell of good coffee among the dew, while colour began to leak back into the day.

I was glad to have stopped. Honesty compels me to the admission that I don't much like casting flies over spawning fish, however exotic they may seem to this Englishman exiled to a Drenthe dawn, and however intrinsically compelling their wanderings may be. There's a part of me which thinks that attempting to catch spawning ide amounts merely to annoying the fish at a critical period of their life. I suspect I'd be ethically more settled trying to outwit them later in the year, when the shoals have migrated back to stillwater again and nose numberously along the stones on a summer's evening. By all accounts ide are to be caught then, too – on small dry flies cast towards the tiny rings which form the ide's rise to midges and other aquatic insects.

I sat on in the dawn, watching the light become a flood

while Rudy's casting image dwindled downstream. There was birdsong, too – a chaffinch defying the rumble and rumours of the noise of the weir, a thrush, a blackbird high in a hazel – and the first dog walkers. Tiny roach sipped at the surface down the edge of the incipient lilies. I kept watching Rudy's shadow downstream. He'd attached his landing net to his jacket with its handle downmost. It hung there like a spare tennis racquet. Suddenly, perhaps because of this image of a man with a net on his back, perhaps simply because of the elegance and economy of his movements, or perhaps simply because I was sitting so comfortably under a tree, the scene acquired a resonance and a depth which was profoundly reassuring. We were, at last, two men who may after all have caught nothing but who were nevertheless outside in a lovely spring dawn. We weren't just fishing. Held there by the spell of the ide, we were going a-angling.

26

16th April 2009
The perils of fly-casting

In 2008 I decided, only 40 years too late, to take some fly-casting lessons. The motives were mixed. First, after 2003 I began to travel fairly widely in search of predatory fish including pike, sea-trout and sea-run charr, and here and there I'd encountered immensely skilled fly-fishers whose techniques put my own to shame. Second, writers visiting prestigious angling places with a view to writing about them ought (I thought) to have what is at least a robust fly-casting repertoire at their disposal. Last, fly-casting is in technical terms interesting, since a viable, replicable set of abilities allows you to fish in places, and over particular fish, which would be out of both reach and range of the standard overhead cast. I joined up, therefore, with a fly-casting course for 20 participants hosted by members and instructors of the North Netherlands Fly-Fishing Society.

The first thing I learned was that there was to be an exam. If you passed the exam, you were to get a nice certificate. That made me gulp a bit. I suppose I'd wanted to appear effortlessly skilled from the start, without putting those putative skills to the test at the end. Then, second, I looked at the technical requirements for the successful completion of the course. If I'd gulped manfully at the idea of an exam, I was left dry-throated by the specific requirements: roll-casting forehanded and back-handed; double-hauling (25 yards with a 5-weight); reach casts; bow casts; parachute casts; casting at targets; casting not at targets; wide loops, narrow loops, tight loops, loops with a rainbow-coloured kink in them and extended, air-mended loops on designer drugs.

It was hugely fortunate that I was able to practice both in my own back garden (casting a fly eight yards onto a handkerchief spread on the lawn or bending a 4-weight line around the apple tree) and on the local reach of canal (parachute casting with the same 4-weight gear over tiny rudd, all of which appeared resolutely unimpressed by the exercise but occasionally took a size 18 barbless dry fly out of nothing more than pity).

I'm afraid I was a trial to my tutors, since on learning or refining each new type of cast I'd ask about its angling utility. What exactly was the parachute cast for? I imagined that it had been designed so that a dry fly would alight softly, but in fact the more practical reason was that a high parachute cast throws at least 3 yards of slack into the fly-line, so that the dry fly is allowed to drift drag-free if cast downstream over, say, rising grayling. And the bow cast? There again, I imagined that the bow cast allowed you to cast a fly around a bush, a rock, an apple tree... But of course, the truer and more practical reason for the existence of such a cast is that it can be used to slow the travel of the fly when one is casting across stream: a bow cast, that is, is a sort of prior upstream or downstream mend made before the line and fly alight. And tight loops? There again...

I was to learn in practice on a lovely reach of the Wylye about tight loops. I'd imagined that the primary function of a tight loop on the backcast was to put speed into the line and therefore allow you to cast further. There on the Wylye, however, I was confronted with the following: I was kneeling on the left bank of the water and casting upstream; behind me, at head height, was a wooden fence topped with barbed wire; spreading over my head, and with its lower branches bending towards the wire on the top of the fence, was an innocent tree. To present the fly to those trout I could see feeding in the green shade near the far bank of the stream I would need to avoid both fence and tree and project the fly 12 yards. The fly had to land very softly, too.

I had two choices, as I saw them then: (a) a roll-cast, (b) a tight-looped back-cast which would slide the fly with great speed and precision between the barbed wire (top of the fence) and the branches (bottom limbs of the tree). A roll-cast was unfeasible since I was kneeling on a high bank. The only option, then, was the ultra-tight loop.

As it happened I got three of those trout, the best going a shade under 2lbs, and I've rarely in technical and angling terms been more satisfied. (Had I known about it at the time, though, I had a third option – a back-hand switch-cast, a kind of single-hand Spey-in-miniature. And yet I was then, and have so far remained, almost totally ignorant of Spey casting. Spey casting, particularly Spey casting with a double-handed rod, is still to come.)

The point of that little experience on the Wylye, and indeed of the first-level casting certificate, was control. It wasn't casting vast distances with shooting-heads; it wasn't how you looked, or what you wore, or showing off. It was merely ...rhythm, dexterity, timing: basic control. You'll have found the same if ever you've taken a gun-dog for its first training lessons. You imagine double-blind dummies, running birds, spectacular retrieves at great distances, field trials, handshakes, money and admiration. What your trainer wants you to do is teach the dog to walk properly to heel and above all to be steady. Trust; quietness; control – these count for far more than speed or showiness.

In September 2008 I took the fly-casting exam and gained the certificate which now hangs almost but not quite ignorably in the smallest room in the house. Typically, I was silently proud and equally typically, I thought I had no more of the basic fly-casting stuff to learn. I was, after all, a *gecertificeerd werper* – and I've been called far worse. Then I met Rudy.

Last week, while fishing unsuccessfully for ide, I had a very close look at Rudy's fly-casting technique, which is accurate and apparently effortless. He was using self-made 3-weight gear and there was one cast he habitually employed which looked spectacularly useful, since it allowed him to pick a dry fly off the water 12 yards to his left and place it immediately 12 yards to the right –without false casting. I asked him to show me. 'Oh yes,' he said, 'it's the CAD cast.' The...? 'The CAD cast – Covers All Directions.' In the CAD cast, he explained, the rod's raised, the fly is picked off, then – rather as in a single Spey – the tip of the fly-line is allowed to touch the water somewhat in front of the caster, then the forward cast is made in the new direction. The effect on the watcher is to see the construction of a precisely timed and circling loop of line; the result is a radically efficient way of presenting the fly at close quarters.

'Yes,' said Rudy. 'The CAD cast… It's great, isn't it? It's almost as useful as the switch cast or the double-circle. And then there's the Viper cast, of course…' The double-…huh? The Viper…?

He showed me enough to show up my basic-level fly-casting certificate for what it is. Like any great teacher, he made me realise how much there was still to learn and how useful it could be to learn it. And so it was back to the lawn, the apple tree and the local rudd. The rudd, however, are still resolutely unimpressed by the perils of fly-casting, chief of which is no more and no less than addiction.

27

20th April 2009
Butterflies and homesickness

My sixth decade seems to have brought with it the realisation of how little I know. I don't mean that I spend the days reciting a woeful *Litany for the Unwitting* and tearing my hair. I do mean that often enough, the things I'm watching, hearing and trying to understand drive me back to the reference books. Take butterflies, for instance. Although my entomology is usually reliable enough to be able to distinguish many common species of insects found on or around the water, particularly where those insects are regularly eaten by trout and grayling, I'm not at all confident about identifying insects not regularly eaten by fish – such as, for example, the different species of butterfly.

For the past three weeks, no drop of rain has fallen in this northerly part of Groningen. The spring sun has done its stuff in a cool spendour. Occasionally during the afternoons it's been warm enough to work shirtlessly outside; so dry has it been that in the evenings I've resorted to the garden hose and the sprinkler on thirty head of lettuce. As the year has warmed, the garden has begun to fill not only with the songs of the arriving summer migrants such as blackcaps and chiffchaffs but also with butterflies, whose lovely Dutch name is *vlinders*.

The earliest arrivals are medium-sized insects with vivid green-yellow wings. I turned to a Dutch reference book first, the *ANWB Natuurgids* (2002): this early arrival is the *citroenvlinder* (*Gonepteryx rhamni*). I subjected *Gonepteryx rhamni* to an English field guide (*Kingfisher Field Guide to the Wildlife of Britain and Europe*, ed. Michael Chinery, p.228.), and there found 'Brimstone'. The British guide told me that the Brimstone appears commonly in the early spring, having overwintered as an adult. It remains in evidence in gardens and along the edges of heath- and woodland until July.

I wondered why brimstones were called what they were. The word *brimstone* is very old, and has cognates in all the Germanic languages. Ultimately, the two elements of the word relate to 'burn' and 'stone' (late Old English [12th century] *brynstan*). *Burn+stone*? 'Formerly the common vernacular name for sulphur...' (OED) – and thus, one supposes, a word transferable to things and creatures possessing the property of being sulphur-yellow: the *brimstone butterfly*, 'an early butterfly with wings of a sulphur colour'. The word is first attested as occurring in its 'butterfly' sense very late in the history of English, in 1827, though it's impossible to believe that the word wasn't in common use many centuries before that.

I lived with brimstones for a week or two and then, last Friday, had an afternoon's fishing down at Baggelhuizen. There was a horrible glitter of sunshine, and a keen wind blew from the north-east, cooling the surface layer and inhibiting any daytime hatch of midges. A few rainbows moved listlessly, pegging about with radical splashes rather than actively feeding. I fiddled with damp Hoppers and dry Hawthorns, though it was still too early for Hawthorns, and caught nothing. Midway through the afternoon I sat on a tree stump at the wood's edge, opened the flask and as I was pouring the coffee, noticed a spectacular pair of wings alight on a nearby thistle-head. Suddenly, the afternoon coalesced into veins, colours and wings. It was as if a randomly panning camera had on the instant stilled and focused.

The butterfly was smaller than the garden brimstones and had white-mottled wings whose tips carried a vivid splodge of orange. Trying to characterise it to myself, I thought it was 'a sort of orange-tipped ...' That evening I went back to the reference books. *Oranjetipje* said the Dutch *Natuurgids*. '*Orange-tip (Anthocharis cardamines)*' said the *Kingfisher Guide* (p.231).

As I put by the reference books, at the instant, and quite unexpectedly, I was confronted with intense homesickness.

I'm usually far too busy to bother with feelings of sickness, in whatever variety these come. There's also the fact that I'm no longer certain where the home is which I'm apparently so homesick for. I could make a case, for example, for the west of Ireland or parts of the Scottish north-west; I could make a more sombre case for the post-industrial Victoriana of Manchester. Nevertheless, there beyond geography, beyond the facts of work and even beyond fishing, there's Yorkshire, the county of my birth and schooling and therefore a First Place. On the upper Derwent, for example, while still a schoolboy I began to keep an angling and entomological log. On the river Rye, I took my first fly-caught trout. In the Dales, I learned about Large

Dark Olives, Iron Blues, Blue-winged Olives and the various sedges. Sitting in this study in Usquert, then, and remembering not only the First Places but all the activity and the lexicon they generated, I started to long to be there, not here.

April, for instance – April on the middle reaches of the Wharfe around Kilnsey. The sheep are long past lambing and the river whispers in pale sherry as it turns past Mile House Dub, where at the head of the pool the trout have started to line up to intercept the first flush-hatches of dark olives. Overhead there's a canopy of implausibly vivid emerald green. Lift your eyes briefly beyond the foliage of willow, alder and silver birch and there's the edge of a scarp, a shoulder of limestone and beyond that, a ruined wall leading your eye upward and still upward, onto the slopes and into the fastness whose ultimate meaning is Old Cote Moor, a summit I once reached, for a bet, in twenty minutes from a standing start on the dale floor at Buckden.

If home isn't necessarily the place you are but is somehow a place where you've learned most quietly and simply to be, then the Dales would, on such a homely and plausible ground, be home. At this time of year, in particular, among the spring-waking world in and around the river, then yes, in that home I could, and did, rejoin the winter-paused things, the insects, the flood-shifted gravels, the first trout of the season.

I looked out of the study window at the resolute spire of Usquert church, whose illuminated clock showed hands at almost ten to midnight. 'But this is home,' I thought, bringing my gaze back to the study, the desk, the triple libraries of angling, poetry and the English language. *Yes, this too is home* ... but it's a long way from home.

I tidied up the reference books. Time to walk the dog and get ready for the night. 'Perhaps,' I thought, as I struggled into a pair of boots and collected the dog's lead from its peg, 'perhaps, and despite the confusion it sometimes causes, it's really a privilege to have, or to have had, at least two homes.' After all, I have fishing, books and butterflies to help me into both.

28

2nd May 2009
Gars, sea-trout and Volkswagens

'...grimme gegrundene gāras flēogan...' wrote the poet of *The Battle of Maldon* in 991: there on the banks of the Essex Blackwater, the English levy and the Viking marauders *let the grimly ground spears fly*. The word *gār* – in *Maldon* used in the plural, *gār+as* (spear+s) – is, then, over 1000 years old. It's clearly from this word, 'gar' meaning 'spear', that the garfish, a creature with a spectacular, sword-pointed hunting snout, gets its English name.

In this north-westerly corner of Europe, each year, and usually in late April, the garfish make their appearance in the coastal shallows of the Baltic and the North Sea. It's a rite of apparition and of seasonal change as meaningful as the appearance of the first mayflies. As the sea along the coasts warms from 7°C through to 10°C, the fisherman squints at a tiny disturbance on the surface horizon ... then another ... and another. The water in these disturbances appears briefly to moil. The surface activity isn't a rise but a quiet, unsplashy ruckus, a coil of bodies. Before the angler can say 'garfish', the shoals of gars are moving all around him. If the coastal shallows are clear, on the next cast ten or more garfish can be seen following the lure or fly.

It's significant – at least, it's significant to me, writing these words less than two miles from the shores of the Wadden – that gars are a prized fish in this part of the Netherlands. Any number of different sources, written and electronic, attest to the importance of garfish both to the angler and the ecology of the areas in which they're encountered. One source (http://www.zeeinzicht.nl/vleet/content/nl) also points out that the shallow, muddy waters of the Wadden Sea provide a haven for young gars (*kinderkamer* – nursery – is the term used), noting that the juveniles spend their first winter in this sheltered, food-rich environment, where they feed on shrimps. In their second and third years these garfish appear to move between the Atlantic west of the British Isles and the Wadden, to which they return in late spring and summer each year, spawning in their third and subsequent years. Significantly for the angler, the same electronic source indicates that Dutch garfish are usually caught at much smaller sizes (averaging 40cm in length) than those encountered in the Baltic. Presumably the Baltic is an even more food-prolific environment than the Wadden and therefore the fish grow more quickly. In both the Wadden and the Baltic, and probably because summer feeding

119

is carried out in such relatively sheltered environments, garfish are surprisingly long-lived – up to 18 years.

The gars we encountered on Funen earlier this week were by Dutch standards massive fish, averaging 70cm and weighing 1lb and more. Up in the clear waters of Langø, on the northerly tip of the island, we encountered shoal after shoal under a high sun and in a light easterly wind which made fish-spotting remarkably easy. The gars would follow our standard sea-trout flies on every cast and seemed particularly attracted to those artificial flies with pink or orange in their make-up. The result of the gars' avid interest was occasionally, and unfortunately, a foul-hooked fish. It was only when we changed patterns to size 12 and 14 flies – again, flies with fluorescent orange in them – that we began to hook the gars properly. The problem of hooking lies in the wonderfully intricate construction of the gar's predatory snout: while it hunts, it attempts to secure its prey side-on, to seize it crossways. A large hook, therefore, will find no purchase on or in the gar's beak. By contrast, a smaller fly can be seized and then, as the fish moves forwards and the current rushes towards its mouth, the fly will be drawn into the mouth cavity. I add only that the fly-fisher shouldn't strike at the first touch of the fish. Wait till the line tightens.

Up at Langø, it didn't seem coincidental that the annual appearance of the garfish had coincided with the arrival of the first shoals of sandeels. Wading back from the coastal reefs through the shallows, for instance, over the sand you'd sometimes see an aquaeous, moving cloud composed of thousands of fleeing eyes.

It wasn't just the garfish which were attracted to the sandeels. Sea-trout were present, too, and one of the most exciting moments of the past week came while I was wading waist-deep and scanning a small reef in which were three patches of open sand. There – no, there! – drifting lazily over a patch of sand was a sea-trout, a massive fish which was certainly 75cm, possibly bigger. Not long afterwards, ten yards uptide, I spotted another. I cast the Pink Pig towards them – of course I did – but they had no interest, and as I retrieved the fly from these careful, tense and unavailing efforts the garfish would sight it, follow it, and try to take it. However lovely the gars might have been, I fished through anticlimax.

It was one of my friends on Funen who explained the local interaction between gars and sea-trout. I was complaining that after the gars arrived the sea-trout seemed to disappear. 'Oh, the sea-trout are there, all right,' he said. 'In fact, they lie under the garfish. Remember that the garfish is a sort of Ferrari, equipped aquadynamically...' (I loved 'aquadynamically', and stole it on the spot) '... aquadynamically for sudden acceleration. By contrast, the sea-trout is a sort of Volkswagen camper...'

Soon after I'd stolen *aquadynamics* I went out one evening to Dalby bay, my mind running with garfish and sea-trout, Ferraris and VWs. I started at the top of the bay's curve, in a vile, squally east wind, and began to pull gars almost immediately. Since I was using a sea-trout pattern, size 6, I didn't react with the rod-hand to any swirl, pull or twitch. 'Ferraris everywhere...' Another swirl, a hint of silver, the line tightening... I didn't react. 'Damn garfi...'

It was a sea-trout, and at 21 inches (53cm) and 3½lb. a decent fish. 'Yes,' I thought in total self-congratulation. 'Worked that one out. Sea-trout lying under the garfish, you see. Absolutely. Just wait for the sea-trout to appear, give them time to take. Oh yes. Sandeels, obviously. Of course. Sandeels. The sandeels are the key... Well done, me.'

I autopsied that 3½lb-er two hours later. Sandeels? There wasn't a sandeel in sight. And although the sea-trout had taken a shrimp-suggesting Pink Pig (size 6), it was full to the gills with ragworms.

29

10th May 2009
Of frogs and fly rods

One of the things that continually reconciles me to living in this northerly and remote part of the Netherlands is the fact that children still play outside instead of wandering around with something electronic glued to their heads. By 'playing outside' I don't mean that they kick balls around; I mean that they construct games whose nature and whose imaginative boundaries they themselves determine. They have dens; build rafts; have string and jamjars. Perhaps as a consequence, they also say Hello, politely, to adults. They are outward-looking and appear generally non-neurotic. Probably, while fiddling about with feathers, sticks and buckets, they aren't unhappy. They remind me of long ago and of a self I once almost forgot.

Two weeks ago I was walking the dog through the copses which surround Usquert Tennis Club. In one of the copses is a ditch spanned by a wooden footbridge. At the bottom of the ditch is a ginnel of unpromising, murky water in which the petals of billions of single-celled algae were already beginning to bloom. In another month, the water in the ditch will be a sullen sludge of emerald. It's here, among the mud and algae, that frogs spawn. Already the fringes of the shallows were full of a translucent slop which held millions of eyes and incipient tails.

Three boys were crouching at the edge of the ditch. One of them had a small net, and another was clutching a bucket in the form of an empty, two-litre paint container.

They looked up when they saw the dog coming. 'She'll do nothing to you,' I said. 'Don't worry. What are you catching?'

'*Kikkertjes.*' Little frogs.

There was a pause while Tess looked into the bucket. There was nothing there apart from some liquid mud and a lonely, algae-smeared twig.

'The frogs are fast, though,' one added.

'The frogs in Usquert are like lightning,' I said (a sentence which taxed the limits of my Dutch).

'And Janko is frightened of frogs. He won't go in and catch them. But they won't bite, will they, mister?'

I told them that frogs had never been known to bite, except perhaps on the Amazon, where – it was well known – there was a race of giant, killer frogs, each one of them the size of a horse.

They was another pause while they digested the horse-sized Amazonian frogs.

'Can the dog help us catch them?'

I told them that Tess was indeed a retriever but that if the frogs were too quick for them, then they'd almost certainly be too quick for Tess.

'Can *you* help us catch them, then?'

I'm not used to talking to strange children. In England, as in many places of a world which has turned even more suspicious than usual, it's simply unwise for a middle-aged man to address a child of unknown provenance. In that world, no one is ever innocent.

'I'd love to, but I'm already late,' I lied.

The dog and I walked on. The boys went back to their net and bucket, and Usquert's uncatchable frogs. A chaffinch sang its heart out on the topmost bough of a lime tree. Somewhere, the mainstay of a flagpole plinked against metal. Somewhere else entirely, a small boy is walking with his sister towards a ditch which lies among fields at the back of Old Tan House, their home in the north of England.

The girl is my middle sister, Sandy. The ditch is an incipient stream which eventually trickles into the River Aire. The boy is a five-year-old me. He's carrying a crabbing net pillaged from a seaside holiday. There are jam jars, buttercups, the sweet stink of cowshit. There, in that place of utter concentration, we caught minnows and put them into the jam jars. We turned over stones and found the match-sized cases of caddis – sedges. We found things that wriggled and things that remained in cautionary stillness. We found the structure of another, intricate world.

These days, people occasionally ask me where fishing began, and I know that my fishing, and all its preoccupations and absorptions, began forty-five years ago in those fields behind Old Tan House. In the world of the crabbing net were creatures with strange names and equally wonderful habits; there was a savage, focused tranquillity whose purposes were eating and reproduction. Crucially, it was a world whose structure and whose limits could possibly, given time and enchantment, be explored and even understood. It was a world in which one could be awake, aware and even, merely as an observer, in place. Beyond all the distances of adulthood, disappointment and failure, it was that world which I brought with me into adult life. The only difference is that the crabbing net has become a fishing rod – an implement with which to divine, to explore, to dowse the invisible and make it shockingly current, live and real.

It's not just fishing. I could never tell this to an audience at a reading – it would sound over-long, abstract and disingenuous – but writing began there, too. That intricacy, all the life lying beyond the green plastic net and the rusted metal of the net-frame had a structure. That is, life in ditches, on seashores, in lakes and rivers behaves non-randomly. There are preferences, habits, seasonal migrations. All of it has a structure, a rhythm which compels some attempt at understanding how it all fits together, an attempt to explore behaviour within pattern.

It was a delight in pattern which brought me to poetry, and

that delight has stayed with me throughout life even though the poetry has been intermittent. At the same time, to be aware of pattern means knowing, explicitly or tacitly, the limits of the pattern: nowhere in either the natural or the unnatural worlds can there be a pattern without constraints. Yet it's the writer's job to explore precisely those constraints, to identify boundaries and if necessary, to go beyond them into the ache, joy and difficulty of new ways of seeing and saying – which, it may be, are new ways of thinking.

Crabbing net, paint bucket, jam jar, fly rod and pen: they are ways to connect, a means to understand, a habit of challenging limits. In my life, these things have amounted to almost half a century of radical time, and all its instants began in a ditch.

I thought back to Janko and the others, and all the *kikkertjes* they were failing to catch. I thought back, too, to the boy who was me, and all the poems he would never write. All alike, though, set in that natural world among whose constraints we are all participants, it makes no sense to ask whether, as frog-catchers, writers or fly-fishers, we were right or wrong.

We were intrigued creatives.

We were held, spellbound, by the edges of understanding.

We are profoundly innocent.

30

20th May 2009
Hedges, flying hooks and Saints' Days

When I lived in Britain and Ireland, the angling and writing year used to have certain friendly and useful rhythms: the university's spring vacation, between Lent and Summer terms, coincided with hatches of Large Dark Olive; late May, and a pause between the end of teaching and the beginning of exams, coincided with the appearance of the Mayfly; the summer vacation took me to the Scottish and Irish wests and to sea-trout; and Reading Week, somewhere in October, coincided with the best of the grayling fishing.

In the early 1990's, the monkeys took over the temporal zoo. Terms became semesters. Tenure was scrapped. From its expansive independence as a profession, university work dwindled into what was merely a job. There was no more free time – or if there was free time, it was (we were told) to be devoted to the getting of money. This was, apparently, our duty.

These days, transposed into exile, the working rhythms are different. April 1st, which I still ring wistfully in the diary, no longer marks the traditional opening of the Yorkshire trout season; the Irish Mayfly are hundreds of miles and two sea-crossings away; and Dutch grayling, like Dutch sea-trout and salmon, could probably be numbered on the fingers of two hands. Instead, I look forward to the first rumours of bass arriving off the coast in IJmuiden, to the appearance of spawning ide in the headwaters of streams, and to the last Saturday in May, which marks the beginning of the Dutch fishing season for perch and zander.

Nevertheless, across time and change there are also some benevolent continuities. A week ago, for instance, I was walking home with the dog one warm, still afternoon and suddenly found myself surrounded by flying hooks. I paused, looked up, and squinted westerly and lengthwise down a line of foam caught in branches It was a hawthorn hedge, fifty yards of blossom. It looked like discarded icing which had been piped in froth onto a gigantic pastoral wedding cake. In the lee of the froth, as it were, was a disorganised squadron of flying hooks: hawthorn flies – *Bibio marci*, so-called because the flies were traditionally thought to appear at or around St.

Mark's Day, April 25th.

If they refer to them at all, Dutch anglers refer to hawthorn flies as *Bibio's* (complete with what appears to English eyes to be an errant apostrophe but which is regularly written in the formation of some Dutch plurals). There is, indeed, a similarity between the hawthorn flies which appear in late April and May and the heather fly, which is a later insect and which the artificial fly called the Bibio represents. The heather fly, however, is an insect I associate with the European north-west, with Scotland or Ireland, and it's not coincidental that the artificial fly, the Bibio, was designed in the last century by Major Charles Roberts, the former owner of the great salmon and sea-trout fishery at Burrishoole in County Mayo. *Bibio marci*, the true hawthorn, hatches in the vicinity of its eponymous bush in later April and May, so it is both earlier than the heather fly and has a slightly different structure, its curved profile and prominent, hairy legs being the most overt of the differences.

In this part of the Netherlands, as in many rural places across north-west Europe, the hawthorn is one of the commonest trees, found abundantly at the edges of fields and pasture. I wondered why this was so. It appears that the hawthorn was widely cultivated and distributed in the 17th and 18th centuries. Herbert Edlin (*The Observer's Book of Trees*, 1975, p.67) for instance points out that at the time of field enclosures in England, constructing boundaries from stone was rare (except in the Yorkshire Dales and parts of the Cotswolds) since stone was so scarce; further, building-quality stone was needed at the same period to provide materials for radically expanding towns, cities and roads. For the farmers of the same period, making field boundaries from wire was too expensive and – then as now, one imagines – uncertain. The farmers therefore resorted to natural materials to construct their fences and boundaries, chief among those materials being the hawthorn, which grew quickly, was satisfactorily prickly and was relatively easy and cheap to maintain. By a happy accident, therefore, so many miles of hawthorns, which were maintained and kept to a viable height by being annually lopped, provide shelter for the hawthorn fly, which is an insect which thrives on damp grassland. In any wind, though, the flies are blown from their shelter and fall onto the surface of any adjacent water, where they are easy pickings for trout – or in the present Dutch context, for miniature rudd and roach.

The hawthorn has been known as an angler's fly for many centuries. If the 'Black Louper' of the 15th century *Treatise of Fishing* is to be identified with the hawthorn, as most recently Fred Buller and Malcolm Greenhalgh have suggested (*Dame Juliana: The Angling Treatyse and its Mysteries*, 2001, pp. 161 and 168-9), then hawthorn representations have been used to catch fish for almost six centuries. Admittedly, the dressing given in the *Treatyse* for the Black Louper is somewhat odd, since it featured 'wings of the red capon with a blue head', leaving the puzzler to wonder whether it was the fly itself which was dressed with a blue head or whether the fowl from which the feather was taken had 'a blue head'. However, for the 15th century author to stipulate a particular kind of blue-headed red capon as the source of the feather fibres would be inconsistent with the generally helpful instructions that same author gives elsewhere in the famous list of twelve flies, and so I follow Buller and Greenhalgh in thinking that the fly itself was tied with a blue head – possibly blue-grey (rabbit?) fur or possibly with blue-grey herls taken from a feather of the same red capon which supplied the wing materials of the artificial (and see Buller 2001, p.169).

The alignment of artificial flies with Saints' Days is a significant feature of the 15th century author's work. He (or she) suggested using 'the tandy fly' – possibly a late Mayfly, or perhaps a Large Summer Dun – at St. William's Day (8th June) and 'the shell fly' – possibly some kind of sedge – at St. Thomas's Day (July 3rd). The author would not have done so, of course, if such Saints' Days could not be used as a convenient angling mnemonic. In other words, such feast days must have been so often and so thoroughly observed as to be able to function as significant pieces of punctuation in the flow of the annual, imaginative landscape.

This year, the hawthorn came late to us. On a recent, rare trout-fishing trip at the beginning of this month I failed to see a single specimen and it was only during the second and third weeks of May that the insect became apparent. This is consistent with my earlier records for the appearance of the fly after cold winters. On 19th May 1985, for example, I enjoyed some good trout fishing at Tittesworth in Staffordshire, using small Black Gnats 'specifically … as a representation of a Hawthorn …' In some subsequent years, the hawthorn

129

season overlapped with that of the Mayfly, giving six weeks' wonderful fishing from late April to the beginning of June.

Those seasons of angling time now lie firmly in my own past and I doubt I shall ever again experience, say, a fortnight's trout fishing on a good stream during hawthorn time. Meanwhile, although the hawthorn bushes survive – straggling into unlopped and untended trees lining many rural lanes in the provinces of Groningen and Drenthe – the universities have lost their Michaelmas, Lent and Summer terms and an increasingly secular Europe is busy forgetting its Saints' Days.

Bibio marci remains; the Black Louper, in some form or another, lives on; but the old temporal and religious rhythms, and all their imaginative reassurances, are gone.

31

1st June 2009
Estranged by the familiar

For almost two years after we moved to Usquert, my boat, which I used to keep at Vinkeveen just south of Amsterdam and in which I used to fish up to three times a week, lay upside-down behind the new house. The oars were laid across rafters in an outhouse ceiling; the outboard was serviced, wrapped in oiled rags, and stored; the portable fish-finder was disconnected from its batteries. I felt as if I'd been disconnected with it.

In April this year, after much deliberation, two kind friends and I trailered the boat down to the Hoornsemeer, south of Groningen. By repute this is the only lake near here which offers interesting pike fishing. (The Lauwersmeer, to our west, holds zander and some pike, but I'd need a bigger and safer boat to venture such an inland sea.) Since April, however, the predator season has been closed, and I've been so hard at work that I haven't had time to take the boat out for an exploratory trip … until today.

Dutch angling law appears to be flexibly applied when it comes to the closed seasons for pike and zander. In strict terms, the zander season closes on March 31st and opens again on the last Saturday of May. In equally strict terms, the pike season closes on February 28th and opens on July 1st, though some local clubs implement their own rules, which may set back the opening day into September or even October. Generally, however, and since the methods used to catch pike are sometimes all but identical to those used to catch zander, many fishers remain busy with their pike fishing into March, or at least until the pike show overt signs of spawning. Equally, many fishers open their pike seasons on 31st May, under cover, as it were, of fishing for zander. Thereafter, some of us experience what are often two or three weeks of very good pike fishing until the surface water warms to 20°C. At and above that temperature, not only does the pike's appetite diminish, but also any hooked pike may be quickly and uncomfortably stressed by the play. Time was when I fished for pike all summer on Vinkeveen, a deep lake where the pike had access at all times to cooler water. I'd always fish either into and beyond dusk, or better still, in the summer dawn when the lake was at its coolest. These days, however, I tend to fish for pike for a mere fortnight or three weeks when the predator season opens and then leave them alone until September, which can be a very good month for big fish.

Three days ago I assembled pike gear suitable for the wide spaces and long drifts of a relatively big lake. I powered the fish-finder; cleaned the drogue; wiped the polarising glasses with a moist cloth and sharpened a selection of jerkbaits and softbaits.

At 0350 the alarm button was blearily jabbed off. I grabbed half a cup of coffee and then drove south. To my left, to the east, the rising sun was first a purple stain on the dark, then a red-rimmed purple, then an orange-rimmed red. I was afloat by 0515, in a northerly wind so light that the Hoornsemeer perch were visibly and audibly moving to pin-fry in a ripple that was no more than a minor corrugation.

Where do you begin pike fishing, on a lake unknown to you?

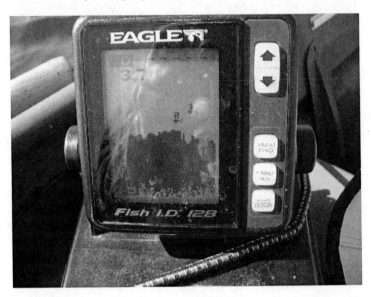

The fish finder I use is a basic Eagle model. It indicates the pixellated presence of fish, true, but far more importantly, it allows me to read underwater contours, weedbeds and other bits of structure such as mussel beds and sunken fences. When I'm hunting pike I look for weed beds, particularly spreading, fish-harbouring beds of *potamogeton* – pondweed. Such weed beds shelter pin-fry, which attract perch, which in turn attract…

Next, I look for drop-offs, places where the bottom of the lake shelves from, say, three feet into six and more feet. While I'm looking for drop-offs I also look for any irregular contours underwater, places which pike can use as lies from which to ambush prey.

Next, I pay particular attention to harbours, sheltered bays with boat houses, stone or wooden jetties.

Next, I cast over points of islands and headlands, and make sure I prospect into any inflowing or outflowing channels.

Always, I keep my eyes open for gulls and terns, which at this time of year are often active at dawn, working over – and diving onto stragglers or cripples from – the shoals of pin-fry on which the perch are hunting. I also look for grebes, especially grebes which are themselves fishing.

In summary, then, when searching a 'new' lake for pike I look, more or less in this order, for weed beds; drop-offs; structure; points and channels ... and for fishing birds. I also keep in mind those most insightful words of the writer and fisherman Paul Gustafson: the pike, he once wrote, are like the lions of the Serengeti; they're never far from their prey.

On the Hoornsemeer this morning I looked, motored, drifted, looked again – and failed to find. There were apparently few weed beds out in the open water, which was a monotonous 3-4 metres deep with relatively few underwater humps and irregularities. The lack of weed is probably caused by the fact that the Hoornsemeer, while clear enough to make fishing jerkbaits and streamers a realistic proposition, is nevertheless a great deal more turbid than Vinkeveen, whose clarity admits light which, of course, helps the weed to flourish.

I found some minor hollows and bumps underwater. Where I found them, I fished them – and usually fished them twice, once with a surface-running jerkbait and once, more deeply, with a rubber shad. I caught nothing. The sun, clearing the orange stain left on the eastern horizon, rose into a flawless, blue-eggshell sky.

I drifted over the points of islands, cast into channels. Time passed. The day came to consciousness, only to find that it was a public holiday and could go back to sleep in the heat.

Far away on the east shore, early-morning dog-walkers were succeeded by a shift of sunbathers.

Here and there on that pleated surface were successive, small swirls. Perch, when predating like this as the warmth leaks into the summer dawn, are in fact interesting and exciting to catch on 5-weight fly-fishing gear and small (size 8-10) Poppers or alternatively on small (size 0) copper or silver Mepps spinners. They also taste delicious when barbecued.

Memories came back this morning as I fished. Barbecued perch; working terns; weed beds, and massive pike taking jerkbaits with a savage water-whorl the size of a tractor tyre; a mottled flank tearing the summer dawn into a white-edged wave cleft by fins; droplets running down lenses; prisms of light… But that was on another lake and in a different time. On the Hoornsemeer this morning I was doing all the old, accustomed things but realised again that for any angler, lakes take time to understand. To work out even some of the pike lies on Vinkeveen, for instance, took me two years, and that was with the help of the fish finder. The Hoornsemeer, though smaller, is in its own way no less complex, and as I backed the boat into its mooring – surprising a spawning shoal of gigantic bream as I did so – I reflected that I still had much to learn and had, in truth, been estranged by the familiar.

32

8th June 2009
Four different names for sand: a visit to Borkum

Borkum is a small and resolutely German island lying off the north-eastern Dutch coast. The slow but Teutonically clean and punctual ferry from Eemshaven (NL) takes 40 minutes to get there over the shallow, silty waters of the Wadden Sea. Look east, look west and the horizon is always the same size. Clouds build and disperse on the slow rim of the world. Far away under the massive curve of the sky there are pylons and wind farms. Summer terns dive into the grey-green wave. It's a place for visionaries, for the exiled and broken-hearted and for those who would be cured.

It was in the 19th century that Borkum first gained its reputation as a curative resort for the well-heeled. Here the German nobility, following the recommendations of their earnest and royal English cousins, were wheeled into the sea in bathing carriages closed to prying eyes. There were flannels, whiskers, mud baths and compulsory sausages among the curious seals and the attendant physicians. Casinos and restaurants were constructed around the obsessions with salt and bowel movements. Like Scarborough, Bournemouth and Blackpool, Borkum became a resort, and through the 20th century was increasingly patronised by middle classes on their annual holidays and the desperate of all social classes looking for some alleviation of the symptoms of TB. Even today, Borkum seems replete with different therapies. The elderly totter along the seafront at the final perimeter of wellness.

As I stared west from the old lighthouse on Borkum – past the sandy expanse of the still-growing Rottumerplaat and beyond the abandoned island of Rotterumeroog (where in the 18th century the Irish Earl of Clancarty, together with three local women and his personal violinist, found sanctuary of a sort) – I asked myself how the Wadden Sea came to exist, and why it supports the marine life it does. Certainly, I knew our local part of the Wadden as a wintering ground for vast flocks of migrant geese, and had often enough visited Noordpolderzijl and Lauwersoog, but the Wadden stretches from the tip of the Dutch mainland eastward, inshore of a string of islands running along the coast of Germany and then northwards, up to and including the islands lying off the east coast of Denmark. It's a vast area of coastal shallows, flooded saltings and treacherous sands. Where did the sand come from? What forces were once at work to create this muddy margin of Europe?

A splendid book by Toon Fey (*Wadden: Gids voor Liefhebbers* [Wadden – A Guide for Enthusiasts], 2002) explains that the Wadden is in geological terms remarkably young. Its formation began at the end of the last Ice Age a mere 10,000 years ago. As the climate warmed, the polar ice melted; the incipient North Sea grew radically in extent and its waves deposited immense quantities of sand on what had been low-lying fen. Simultaneously, as the ice retreated from north-west mainland Europe, the rivers – chief of them, the Rhine – started to flow, depositing vast quantities of post-glacial rubble into the sea along the northern coasts of Europe. Soon afterwards, the Dover-Calais land bridge was breached, and further powerful currents swept new deposits of sand from the south-east along the Dutch coast.

What is now the Wadden Sea, then, was formed by climate change and a set of post-glacial accidents. It was a slow business: although the last Ice Age ended 10,000 years ago, even 2,000 years ago the Dutch Wadden didn't quite yet exist since its islands-to-come were still joined to the mainland. 1,000 years ago, as North Sea currents tore at the Dutch coast and as the IJsselmeer filled, the Wadden's islands began to appear. By the 13th century, the Dutch coastline, its necklace of northerly islands, and the Wadden Sea to the east, had begun to assume an almost-familiar shape.

The Wadden is still changing. New dunes appear; old mud flats disappear. The nautical charts of the area must be annually renewed. To understand the continual shifts, the cartographer, the shrimp-boat skipper and the onlooker must alike be connoisseurs of sand. As Fey's work describes, in navigating this topography one needs at least four different names for sand: above 2mm and a grain of dirt is referred to as *grind* – gravel; between 0.05 and 2mm a grain is referred to as the familiar *zand*; between 0.02 and 0.05mm one speaks of *silt*; under 0.05mm and a grain of erstwhile silt has become *lutum* (Fey 2002, p.20). Even the process of gully- and dune-forming has acquired different names in Dutch: sand blows along the coast in *kustdrift*; the shallow depressions in sand-drifts are called *zwinnen* and the wet gullies at the bottom of the *zwinnen*, through which seawater runs during the ebb, *muien*. Compared to this Netherlandish lexical precision, the alleged number of different Inuit words for snow makes the Greenlandic dialects seem tongue-tied.

Recently, too, the North Sea has warmed and as it has warmed, fish which even twenty years ago were scarcely found in the North Sea have begun to extend the northern limits of their range. One of these fish is the bass. These days, each summer they spread north from the English Channel towards the eastern Dutch coast, where they're regularly caught on rod-and-line in Zeeland and at IJmuiden. During the later summer months they appear to prospect into the Wadden, where they're caught in the surf on the northern beaches of Vlieland and Ameland. And why would they not do so? This part of the Wadden, warm, shallow and nutrient-rich, harbours an abundance of plankton, shrimp, cockles, mussels and flat-fish. Through July and the rest of the summer, and often as late as October, bass are still caught on Borkum, and there are reliable reports of bass being regularly caught off the west coast of Jutland.

As I stood under the old lighthouse at Borkum, therefore,

I looked at the Wadden with three eyes: the eye of the social historian; that of the topographer and amateur naturalist; and that of the angler. In front of me, along the south-east coast of Borkum, lay a tidal channel and relatively deep water. According to the minimal literature that exists on fishing for bass on Borkum (see for example http://www.borkum.de/index.php?sid=1289), this channel, which is fished from the coast along a series of beach-reinforcing stone jetties (*Buhnen* in German), is a bass mark. Away to the north of the island is another beach, loaded with surf even in a moderate wind, giving on to the North Sea. Here, too, anglers have caught bass, usually on beach-casters rigged with *Wattwurmen* ('Waddenworms' – lugworms). It struck me, as we were pulling away from the dock yesterday at the south of the island, that the strong tidal currents running on the ebb past the ferry terminal might also be worth a cast.

I shall go. Later this summer, once the present run of incessant work, writing and marking is over, I shall go. For the moment, Borkum will become a case of virtual fishing, while I explore the charts and maps and the few records of others. And yes, once the summer has turned into the full and tame sameness of its green, there will as always rise up in my angler's eye images of the coast and the clean west wind, of flood and sea-trout … and of bass, too.

I shall fish out of my own exile, casting a fly among the immensity of post-glacial accident. Out on the mud flats, among the *zwinnen* and *muien* and the running tide, there will be another kind of cure.

33

28th June 2009
Usquert-London, return.

It was a delight to find that we can take the 0759 local train to Groningen from the village station and, travelling via Rotterdam, Antwerp and Brussels, arrive at London St. Pancras eight hours later. A delight, but also an education in cultural geography. The journey begins in this most cloud-lovely and horizon-curving of flatlands, runs south across the Rhine's great westerly arms of the Maas and Lek, southward again towards the pantiles, mellow sunlight and ornate Catholic spires of Belgium, and then veers north-west from Brussels, across and under the northern French chalk, whose every mile is poppies. Here, glimpsed from the train through gaps in modern embankments, there are tench-harbouring pools under willows; abandoned tractors and worked pea fields; ricks and the ridges of low hills. There are wine bottles on tablecloths; a Gauloise abandoned to an ashtray; eels in green stagnancies that border the long miles of crosses.

The tunnel is a sudden dark. Without quite realising it, you're holding your breath. Lights prick on inside Eurostar. The meniscus of your cup of coffee barely simmers as the train speeds under the Channel.

Emerging into sunlight, there's another – the barest – glimpse of Kent before the geography turns ever more utilitarian. There's chrome at Ebbsfleet International. (*'Where?'* asked Monika, with rising intonation that bordered on incredulity.) There's chrome at Ashford International. There's chrome at St. Pancras International, and a high steel roof that cradles unlovely glass tubes no traveller can escape. Here, too, there's the continual sense of being watched, chipped, scanned. Having arrived in England, you become part of the herd that sweats and munches on CCTV.

The transposition from the Wadden to London ran exactly to time, but its end was puzzlement. The city was crammed with multilingual humanity. Since I last visited, in 2005, the great monuments – Cleopatra's Needle, the Westminster clock, the dome of St. Paul's – seem to have been incorporated into some kind of theme-park whose operators are only too happy to take your money but provide you with very few places to sit down, think or rest. Perhaps it was because I was both sleepless and restless that I found it difficult to become a tourist in my own land.

Over the past thirty years, and across what's becoming a liftetime pattern of journeys, I seem to have developed two responses to these recurrent feelings of estrangement. One is to haunt either churches or galleries; the other is to find water. In London, it's impossible to avoid either the haunting or the finding. At the Tower, for instance, there's the semi-submerged entry that is Traitor's Gate, to which important political prisoners (among them, Thomas More) were brought in security and secrecy down the Thames. Elsewhere, even as you walk from Aldwych, for example, towards Trafalgar Square and the National Gallery, you can occasionally, at the end of south-running streets, spy the Thames to your right, a glitter of water at the bottom of your vision.

The crowds, the shoppers, the chains of food outlets peddling wraps and sushi... I heard myself overhearing the memory of T.S. Eliot's lines about death undoing so many as the crowds poured over London Bridge. But in this fragment of the wasteland, the river was still a strong brown god. Nor is it coincidental that the Thames floods Dickens, to the extent that its mists, its snickets and ginnels of gas-lit vapour, its miasmas and drownings, terrible findings and human flotsam constitute what is almost a Greek chorus whose voice is heard in so many Dickens novels. The legal squalors of Jarndyce vs. Jarndyce play out to the eternal commentary of tidal water. As Hilaire Belloc once put it, 'The Thames made London. London is a function of the Thames...' (*The River of London*, p.7)

As we travelled, by water, from the Tower to Westminster I thought, too, of the tributaries of the Thames, London's other rivers. And suddenly, standing there on a tourist boat heading past the reconstructed Globe Theatre, the city and its teeming seemed to recede, and all its sound muted, and there rose up in my mind's eye the image of mud flats at low tide, a marsh containing knolls of low hills, curlews weeping at the slow line hemming the vast inverted bowl of the sky and the horizon's curve within it.

Two thousand years ago, perhaps that was something of how it was. To the north, the other rivers, Thames tributaries, among them the Fleet, ran southwards through the marsh to merge with their brown parent, and then both would travel eastwards to the yellow waters of a North Sea that – not long before, as

141

geological time is reckoned – had been released from ice.

As others – august others – have pointed out, most London tourists have no idea that they are walking over rivers. The other rivers have not been altogether lost. Some, like the Fleet, have been systematised. The luckier of the rivers became canals; the unlucky became sewers. Both sewers and canals were channelled, bricked in, and then offered to the earth underground. From these underground culverts the old rivers now flow into the Thames over shallow runnels of dank concrete. But, miraculously, they are still there.

We got lost two days ago, on our way from Russell Square to Nelson's Column. We strayed towards Holborn – not 'Hol'+'born' but *Hoe-b'n* or even, still more properly, *O-b'n*. Monika looked at me quizzically, suspecting middle-aged pedantry. Yet I hope it's not merely pedantry that delights to remember that *O-b'n* is a reduced, time-worn form of *Old-bourne* – the old spring from which the Fleet originally flowed.

There are other forgotten rivers. The Tyburn runs under Mayfair; the Westbourne flows in pipes under Hyde Park. It's entirely possible that, long ago, all these streams held flounders, trout and eels, and it's just possible that in September and October each year, salmon and sea-trout made spawning runs into the gravels lying at the edge of what is now the London Transport map.

While we sat in St. James's Park and ate ice-creams I tried to reconstruct how it must have been, this historical geography where curlew and dunlin were choreographed by time and greed into conduits. I couldn't do it. The scale of change has been too great, and my imagination is too small. It was as if our Dutch part of the Wadden were to become a city the size of London, and all its canals, mud flats and intricate migrations were to be managed into commerce, traffic and oblivion.

I was still thinking about rivers, mud flats, time,

estrangement and theme-parks when we retraced our route home on Eurostar. *Glimpse of Kent – hold your breath for the Channel – eels, poppies and crosses – red roofs of Belgium ...* It was somewhere around the first poppies that Monika looked up from a German newspaper and silently passed me the page on which it was reported that the Wadden had been named a World Heritage Site. Our local *maren*, therefore, are almost guaranteed never to become an urban sump. As we changed money, identities and trains in Brussels it came as a small relief to think that what remains of our rivers – yes, exiled in Brussels I was thinking of them as 'ours' – will never become a cistern, nor ever flow underground.

34

1st July 2009
Small things.

Het Hogeland is dust-dry. The local farmers, who are complaining about blight, have begun to spray the potato drills. Greenfly infest the climbing roses, and every evening, after the garden is watered, a plague of slugs and snails crawls slowly over the herb beds. I rarely, and then as a last resort, use chemicals on the garden, and can only hope that our resident hedgehog does its nocturnal job, but judging by the numbers of swollen slug bodies I find, it's slacking. Meanwhile, the blackbirds, looking dowdy now, chip away with their beaks at an unyielding and yellowing lawn.

In this culture of heat and dead-heading, dawn and dusk are the only properly habitable time for humans just as they're the only times when the fish are active. Walk down any canal in the hours around sunrise or sunset and you walk into a conspiracy of circles – surface rings which betray the feeding roach and rudd fiddling about just under a water surface made matt with dust. In the shallows adjacent to the main channel, the lilies have started to bloom. Their emerald underwater leaves shelter millions of pin-fry generated by the spawning of two months ago. Nearby, in hollows on the bed of the canal or lying around the wooden and brick structures of bridges and leats, rest the restless perch, their big eyes alert for pin-fry stragglers. There, where a pair of waterhens have made a green nest of twigs resting on the lilies, the algae and string-weed caught in reed stems are disturbed by the back of a small carp as it rootles among the greenery. Late on, as day finally slides into night across the slow rim of the world, there's a shocking, hunting swirl on the far bank: a little pike. The ripples from this brief predatory moment spread to dinner table size, then ebb and subside under the harsh cries of oystercatchers. As the sky bleaches into darkness and the last stricken streaks of red become purple before merging into the machinery of stars, a wave of whispering silence folds across the villages.

Even in the deadening heat at this zenith of the year, the polder is full of life.

I sometimes wonder whether it's ethical to annoy these typically small rudd, roach and perch with a 4-weight. Twice a week, perhaps, I venture out from home around dusk to ply the light fly rod. The fishing's a matter of attention to detail: a greased and relatively long (10-12

foot) leader ending in a point of 7x nylon; degreasing the tip of the leader every twenty minutes; where necessary, de-barbing the tiny hook, which holds a scrap of a fly – a Goldhead or film-fished dry-fly, size 16 or 18; sliding the artery forceps which I use as unhooking pliers into an easily accessible pocket... It's delicacy, lightness and precision.

The fish, and in particular, the rudd of over the half pound, can be as wary as any trout. I creep along the banks in trainers, looking for moving fish. Once I've found a group of such fish – they're feeding on diminutive midge pupae, I think – I stop creeping, and hunker inelegantly. Thereafter, it's a high back-cast (to avoid nettles and fences) and a tight loop, with an upward-aimed forward cast that will mean the line straightens in the air and falls softly. Anything splashy or clumsy will be punished by a sullen water surface under which the fish have simply scattered and have resumed feeding ... elsewhere.

Whatever the books say, I've found that a fly fished under the surface results in many more takes than a floating fly. Tradition, that is, suggests that rudd will take bushy a dry-fly such as a Soldier Palmer. Well, so they might: little rudd can be greedy. Nevertheless, the larger fish seem to take pupae-suggesting patterns far more readily in the dusk. It's as dusk turns to darkness that the fish begin to lose their caution and will take a fully floating artificial. Last night was a good example: starting fishing at 2100, I began to pick up roach immediately, and all of them took a Goldhead, an undistinguished, buff-coloured fragment tied on a size 16 hook. Twenty minutes later, and a small shoal of perch tucked in to the near bank found the Goldhead immensely to their liking, to the extent that I stopped fishing for them after getting a hit from a bristling, angry perch on every cast. It was only at 2210, as the last of the light was leaching from the empty sky,

145

that I changed to a white dry-fly with a stub of red-fibred tail. Cast over a rising roach, this brought an immediate response – a swirl that shrugged at, then annexed the floater. I needed the artery forceps for that one.

It was lovely fishing, but after I'd stopped casting and hunkering and was merely sitting and looking at light draining from high cloud I wondered about the ethics of what I was doing.

In general, I much prefer angling for those fish which in principle I can eat. By this I don't mean I 'fish for the pot'. Since 2000, for example, counted across all species I must have caught well into four figures of fish – pike, salmon, sea-trout, perch, trout of various kinds, charr, grayling, rudd and roach, garfish… Of these, I have killed and eaten fewer than thirty: two pike, four sea-trout, half a dozen garfish, one Greenland charr, half a dozen brown or rainbow trout and half a dozen small perch, which last are excellent when barbecued. I've not killed a Scottish sea-trout, nor have I killed a grayling, for over a decade, and I have never yet killed a rudd or roach for the table. I suspect they would be as tasty as cotton wool.

It's also the case that when I have caught whatever it is I feel I'm there to catch I prefer, these days, simply to stop fishing. A trip to Greenland (2004) was a good instance of this inclination to fill the angling days with creative pauses. The charr – sea-run, often tide-bright beauties running up to 7lb. and bigger – were so abundant that it was a relatively simple matter to catch twenty or thirty of them in half a day. Why persist? The confrontation with such profligacy didn't feel like any sort of angling challenge, and I preferred to wander about with the cameras in bleak, glacial river valleys filled with bones.

And yet in principle, yes, I prefer to fish for those species I can, or could potentially, eat. I ate one of those Greenland charr, and continued to fish with the idea that I *might just*

146

eat another, sooner or, more likely, in a much-deferred and even endless later. I occasionally think I'm fishing for pike on the same basis: each year, I think I *might just* allow myself to kill a small jack so that Monika can embark on the culinary complexities of *quennelles*... But the pike seasons pass, and every pike I'm lucky enough to catch is returned, often via barbless hooks, safely to the water.

All the same, roach and rudd are not edible by any reasonable stretch of the gastronomic imagination. So what am I doing, annoying them with a 4-weight? I think back to an image I've tried to explore many times: the boy with a crabbing net, the boy intrigued by the life that there is in ditches, the boy in conversation with the structure of an outwardly directed solitude. The adult – the man who hunkers on the banks of the polder and plies a Goldhead over dusk-rising roach – has simply replaced the crabbing net with a fly rod. The fly rod is his connection with the intricacies of all the life in, under and around the water which he's trying so radically to understand.

This isn't an age which understands the possible structures of solitude. Solitude, and the desire to understand, can't be taught, don't happen within the illusions of the internet, and can't be called on a mobile. Nor, properly understood, can angling solitude be coerced into a self-generated shape: it's not composed by one's own electronic playlists or 'Favourites' pages, but is filled with strange detail, puzzlement and the compelling needs and timings of the natural world. Angling, in that sense – even angling for 8-inch-long roach and rudd and other small things – includes the profound extravertion which places you outside and includes you in another dusk as the gross world is smothered again in dust and summer darkness.

35

3rd July 2009
The carp virgin.

I can't prove it, but I suspect that here in the Netherlands, fishing for carp is probably the most popular form of rod-and-line angling. Many Dutch waters could, after all, have been designed purposely as carp habitats: slow-flowing or still, they lie under the clouds and gather reflections. Their make and meaning is tranquillity, and within the stillness live intricate forms of plant, fish and animal life. In the heat, thousands of snails drift under the surface in their inert migrations; pin-fry nitter over the green umbrella of a lily pad; perch wait in ambush, bristling with apparent indignation, around the wooden structures that funnel into the stonework of a canal bridge. Overhead, between the clouds and their water-mirror, the air is full of the shrieking of swifts. Below the shrieking, the water has become less a substance than a view.

In July, the year seems to decelerate. *Green*, says the distant prospect where the potato drills are growing. *Green*, says the foliage on the arch of poplars. *Green*, says the hedge which screens the lawn. This is where July has aimed, into greenery and lushness, the year's dead noon. The sharpness and zest of spring have gone. The blackbirds, looking dowdy, have stopped singing. The world has slowed into heat.

Something moves, below the enervation. Walk up almost any canal on almost any warm and still summer evening, and here and there you'll see a lily pad trill inexplicably. Below the silent trilling, the bumping and nudging of reed and weed stem, will be a carp. Occasionally, at the edge of the same lilies, you'll see the water bulge as something turns away underwater: carp.

On the rim of dark, a large swirl begins to spread through the weedbeds at the edge of the canal. The greenery mutes the ripple ebbing from the swirl, and eventually stills it. The canal resumes its reflections, the swifts and martins their shrieking. But what has moved, massive and momentary, will be a carp.

No wonder, then, that fishing for carp has become a multi-million-Euro industry. Camouflage clothing, bivouacs and bed chairs; boilies in natural, raspberry or peanut flavour; wicked hair-rigs, and bolt-rigs on which a carp will hook itself… Carp fishing, and all its accoutrements, has become less a form of angling and more and more comprehends the impedimenta of a rite. Across the Netherlands are rooms full of angling arcana. Carp fishers are a congregation of secular priests.

Perhaps because catching a carp seems, these days, so expensively esoteric, I hadn't tried deliberately to catch a carp for nearly thirty years. On that occasion, using borrowed gear, I hooked and lost a carp which took a free-lined freshwater mussel at the edge of dusk. For almost three decades afterwards I remained a carp virgin. Nevertheless, surrounded now in July's sullen greenery by canals and carp, I resolved to try and catch one on the fly rod.

For all the Dutch angling reports telling me that catching carp on the fly was eminently possible, I doubted that I would succeed. Conditioned by the compulsions of the esoteric, I imagined that I would have to pre-bait a swim, lay plans of campaign that stretched across days (and nights), feed the rumours of the water with dog biscuits or floating crust before a carp would even deign to inspect whatever was on the hook attached to my line.

As it was, the first thing I reached for was a good pair of polarising sunglasses. For what I intended to do it was vital to be able to spot the carp, and carp spotting isn't easy in these polders. They're usually far too turbid for easy fish watching.

On just one or two weeks a year – usually windless weeks during a dry spell – the suspended silts and clays settle, and fish can be spotted. The second thing I reached for was therefore an accurate weather forecast, and if possible, a heatwave. Third, I reached for a 4-weight fly rod, a reel with plenty of backing on it, and some fluorocarbon that would function at the business end of the line. For the record, I selected 0.205mm fluorocarbon as point material – about 5lb. breaking-strain. The carp I'd seen were generally small common carp which ran to low double figures. These are relatively small carp and, with luck, they might be safely landed on lightish tackle. Last, there was the 'fly'. I tied up a handful of what in Dutch are called *zalmeitjes*, salmon eggs. These may have started life as representations of salmon ova, but dressed large onto a strong hook (Kamasan B175, size 6) they look like mutant, fluorescent yellow flakes of Wonderloaf. Fake bread.

I needed sunshine and daylight in order to spot the carp most easily. It was already nearly 30°C and cloudless as I tackled up at 1000. As I pulled the fly-line through the rings I spotted a carp cruising at the edge of lily pads on the near bank. It mooched off into the shadows provided by a massive oak on the far bank, subsiding into darkness on the slowest and subtlest of surface bulges. That was at least promising.

The tackle readied, I waited. Sweat began to form and run. It's surprising how much you can see, if you simply wait by water. The pin-fry fritter about in the shallows; a snail crawls down a stem; waterhen chicks cry piteously from a nest made of algae and twigs; a coot fusses at the hiss of a breeze that is almost silence.

I waited again. It wouldn't be true to say nothing was happening. Plenty was happening, but nothing of angling relevance was included in the nothing that was happening. As the sun rose higher – it was 1055 – I suspected that the carp, which had been visible rumours to begin with, had disappeared rumorously into the rumorous depths, had become merely green thoughts of fish in green depths of shade.

I watched as a lily pad twenty yards away began to trill. A faint but intense ripple issued from the greenery. A stem, and a floating mat of algae, were nudged. Under the trilling and nudging lay a carp, which was rootling about on the underside of the lilies.

I had no idea how to cast the fake bread towards the carp, since the fish lay in thick cover. If I cast directly towards the carp, the fly would sink and then would lodge immediately in the lilies. I was pondering the problem when, very obligingly, the carp appeared from the lily bed, swimming slowly – massively – at an angle towards me. I had one chance to get the cast right, one chance to land the fake bread lightly and accurately in front of (but not too close to) the carp and in its line of vision, one chance ... I took it.

It was a fluke ('a fluke of flake' I registered, as I held my breath). The carp cruised, the fly landed, and ... The carp appeared at first to ignore the slowly sinking scrap of yellow. Then it spotted it, followed it downwards, accelerated slowly towards it and, as the size 6 hook was still sinking towards rumour, took it.

By 1100 the tussle was over, and a common carp of around 6lbs lay in the net. The moorhen returned to its fussing, the waterhen chicks began crying again and the vast shoals of pin-fry reformed under clouds which had rejoined their reflections. I had finally become something other than a carp virgin, and sat sweating in the sunshine, enjoying a post-coital cigarette.

30°C. High summer. The swifts and martins shrieked on, with indifference that seemed like derision.

36

21st July 2009
The haunting of Yeats and terns.

At some time in July a great restlessness comes over me, and I long to get away from the dust and lush greens, the blown and blowsy gardens, the ever-more-silent birds, and travel out to the Irish west and its remote places. As a result, I spent the past week fishing two estuaries in Donegal. Remote these places certainly were: I didn't see another fisherman all week.

The catches were by any standards modest – a dozen small sea-trout up to 1lb. I was multiply gale-blown, continually rained upon. Hands turned into browned, salt-encrusted and storm-scarred appendages. Blisters formed on blisters. I was stung on the neck by something I couldn't identify before I swatted whatever it was. My leather watch strap turned stiff and flaky with seawater. Lips cracked in the sun, salt and wind. Though I fished alone almost throughout the week, I was never for one moment lonely. I was merely isolated, slightly damp and obsessed. It was altogether magnificent.

By an accident I had arranged to stay in a guest house which overlooked an island called Inishfree, and perhaps as a result, I couldn't shake lines from the poet W.B. Yeats out of my head all week. The haunting wasn't so much a matter of his great early poem 'The Lake Isle of Innisfree', though I noted wryly that I did a great deal of arising and going during the course of a short, wet sea-trout trip. Rather, it was a matter of Yeats's poem whose protagonist is the fiddler of Dooney: *When I play on my fiddle in Dooney,/ Folk dance like a wave of the sea*... However and for however long I tried, I simply couldn't rid my brain of these lines – indeed, of the whole poem. As I fished, and was arising and going now, Yeats and his fiddler therefore came with me.

Yeats, the fiddler and I walked and fished among terns. Of all summer migrant birds I love the terns most, largely because they are always and everywhere (at least, everywhere in the Irish west) birds of the clear tidal currents, and those currents hold sea-trout and mackerel while these hunt for the shoals of sandeels, sprit and other prey on which the terns are also predating. A huge, hunting reciprocity governs the push of the tides.

While globally, terns are classified into ten genera and forty-four species, five species are regularly found in this part of Europe. Two of them – the Arctic and the Common tern – I find almost impossible to tell apart on a quick glance, though if I take time I can usually identify the Arctic bird because of its vividly and wholly red beak. The Little tern, on the other hand, is, though rarer, much more easily identifiable because it is ... well, little, a bare nine inches long. The Sandwich tern, whose breast is 'suffused with rose' (Hudson, *British Birds*, 1902, p.322), I'm not conscious of ever having identified, though I'm certain I must have seen it. The Roseate tern I have never seen.

As I watch them, I'm impressed, as always, by the terns' sheer elegance: those angularly folded wings; the ability of the birds to hold station in the buffeting of the wind; their hover...

and that final, precise and unanswerable dive.

I spent much time on this last trip, while trying to rid myself of the presence of Yeats, attempting to find an image for the tern's dive. 'Dive' is in truth a clumsy word: it spans a tuck to a belly-flop, and terns are anything but tucked or floppy. They're light, grace; they are the nerves of the hunting air itself. What, then? A plunge? No. A plummet? Definitely not. A …?

I watched the terns on the Gweebarra estuary; I watched them in the main, moiling channel of tide in Ballyness Bay. As I watched, I tried to reconstruct what I knew of their immense migratory journeys. The Little tern, for instance, overwinters in West Africa. The Arctic tern, as its name implies, may nest in the high north but spends the winter as far south as the South Atlantic, making it the most far-travelled of any bird. It's the Arctic tern, too, which is so fond of sandeels, unlike the Common tern, which one can readily see off the Dutch coasts in summer, feeding on shrimps tossed about in the outfall of the power station at Eemshaven.

When I play …

I tried again for an image of the diving tern, my tired head shadowed by Yeats and terns, journeys and power stations, distances, dust and migration. A force, a drop, a sudden splash …? No. Oh dear me: no.

What must they have seen, these bird-fragments that hunt out of the immensity of the Atlantic winds? The coasts of Argentina and Brazil, waves breaking on the white sands of tropical cocktail; far inland, glimpsed from the endless Latin breakers, the dwindling rainforests; the isthmus of Panama, its neck wrung by ships …

… dance like a wave of the sea …

… and then the long expanse of ocean, the vast corrugations and storm, clouds building vertically and dispersing, the pull of magnetism, the sensed isobars, the cycles of daily dying and becoming – and then a glimpse of land, whitewashed houses straggling up the side-fall of hills, the luminous breakers smoothing into the calm resolution of an estuary where the sandeels are waiting…

I fished on, among abandoned lines, lost images, and sea-trout. Every time I walked back up-tide to where the main channel of Ballyness Bay begins, the terns reeled about in air, and the day was full of indignant, protesting cries as they sensed an unwelcome, alien presence. Out in the current, a seal thrashed about in a scum-lane, shaking a sea-trout in its terrible jaws. To the south, the bared top of the mountain called Erigall gave slopes of quartz and slate back to a sudden fit of fell sunshine.

Clouds lifted and dispersed. In the hours around low water, I caught and released a handful of small sea-trout. The terns followed the sandeels into the ebb.

I left Donegal, driving through cloud bursts and rainbows back to Belfast and from there taking a flight to Amsterdam. At Schiphol, the train to Amersfoort, and from there to Groningen, was jammed with human freight, all of us carrying heavy bags and recent holiday memories. I tried hard to disconnect from overhearing others' mobile telephone conversations by working on images of my own: Donegal, Yeats, sea-trout and terns…

… *And dance* …

Donegal, where …

The tern draws the sky
through the needle of its dive.

37

28th July 2009
Earls and islands.

As I'd promised myself, I went back to Borkum and attempted to catch the rumours that are bass. While the tide flooded down a shoreline spiked with *Bühnen* (croys) I was briefly distracted by a squall of seagulls, each diving onto something the naked eye couldn't see. I thought back ten days to Donegal and diving terns, sea-trout and the clear waters of the Atlantic. In Borkum, the seagulls were working the end of the town sewer. Far from the sage-green tide and yellow-finned trout moving to sprit over white sand, I'd come back to the muds of the Wadden, shit and holidaymakers.

I spent much time casting and retrieving a rubber sandeel and deflecting the questions of excessively fat and curious German children. Eventually, the children went away and the sandeel lodged sullenly in the sea bed. Stifling 'Scheisse', I became patience on a monument and looked westwards out to sea. Riding there in a rain-bearing mist was the restored ruin – a former navigation beacon – which marks the end of the sands on the island of Rottumeroog. Barely discernible in the distance was Rottumeroog's sister island, Rottumerplaat. The last, composed of sand and scrub, is growing in extent as the marram grass takes root and the dunes spread. Rottumeroog, by contrast, is slowly shrinking, and at the same time is shifting eastwards.

It has a strange and spectacular history, this island adrift to time off the north-eastern Dutch coast. In the later Middle Ages, ownership of the island was shared between two local religious foundations. By the 17th century, Rottumeroog had been taken into private ownership, first by a syndicate and then by a succession of notables (inluding notable widows) from the neighbouring village of Warffum. In 1706, however, the island was again sold, this time to Donough Macarthy [or McCarthy], 4th Earl of Clancarty.

The open-access internet pages of *Burke's Peerage* do not detail the history of the Clancarty titles. The earldom has in fact been instituted twice, first in the 17th century and subsequently, after an early 18th century unpleasantness (of which more below), in 1803. Other sources remain tight-lipped, even coy about the life of the 4th Earl, telling us little except the fact that he was attainted in 1691 and was at that time obliged to give up his titles.

The 4th Earl was born in Blarney, County Cork in 1668. Although his family were originally Catholic, Clancarty received a Protestant education on the death of his father and trained as a soldier, becoming colonel of (in one account) an infantry regiment which supported James II in his futile Irish campaign against William of Orange. After William's general, Marlborough, had successfully attacked Cork in 1689, Clancarty was imprisoned in the Tower of London and his Irish estates – worth nearly a quarter of a million pounds – were confiscated. Six years earlier, he had contracted a marriage with the 11-year-old Elisabeth Spencer, daughter of the influential Duke of Sunderland.

Clancarty escaped from the Tower in 1694 and assumed the command of a platoon of Irish rebels in France. This came to nothing. After the Treaty of Rijswijk (1697), which offered some hope of reconciliation between former Protestant and Catholic enemies, he returned to London and a belated beginning to married life, but almost immediately was turned in to the authorities (by his brother-in-law) and again imprisoned in the Tower. After a petition for clemency he was exiled, with a pension of 300 pounds a year, on the stringent condition that he should never set foot in Great Britain again.

He drifted, accompanied by his wife. A restless stay north of Groningen was followed by another restless stay in Altona, near Hamburg. Houses were bought, exchanged, abandoned. His wife died in 1704. She was 31 years old, and far from home. In 1706 Clancarty bought the island of Rottumeroog from Abel Eppo van Bolhuis, a Warffumer.

Clancarty reminds me of a friend I used to drink with. In any bar, the friend would invariably take a seat with his back to the wall, facing the door and close to an exit. He wanted to see what kind of human was approaching him. Enraged husbands, for example; bailiffs serving divorce papers; bank officials... The friend, seeing or even merely sensing the arrival of an unwelcome face, would often disappear in the middle of a sentence. Sometimes he'd disappear in the middle of a phrase. Occasionally, he wouldn't come back for hours. At last, he didn't come back at all.

The same punctilious nervousness seems to mark Clancarty's preference for living near the sea. On an island, every potential visitor can be scrutinised by sail in advance, and equally, an exit is possible in almost any direction.

He didn't lack style. Local people called him 'de malle graaf' – the eccentric earl. It is certain that he took three local women to the island as companions – one a red-head, one a brunette, and one a blonde. Less certain is whether he took to Rottumeroog a personal violinist, or whether – as in Reinder H. Postma's account (*Donough McCarthy*, 2007), to which I'm greatly indebted – his musical entertainment was provided by a group of musicians from Hamburg.

He was suspected, probably with justice, of piracy, and it's at least highly likely that this exiled Irish earl, who had once as a young man entertained the King of England and had exchanged vows with his child bride in Westminster Abbey, lived a tenuous, even tramp-like existence on Rottumeroog. In 1717, after a severe storm on Christmas Day, Clancarty abandoned the island together with his mistresses, one of whom subsequently gave birth to a son who died in infancy and was buried in Warffum church.

The *malle graaf* retained ownership of Rottumeroog until 1731. During his tenure, or perhaps because of it, the island fell into neglect. He passed his final years in the hinterland of Schleswig-Holstein. Donough Macarthy, 4th Earl of Clancarty, died in Altona in 1734. The fate of his remaining mistresses, and of his musicians, is nowhere recorded.

I was still thinking about Clancarty and his restless, largely exiled and peripheral life as the ferry brought me back across the Wadden after a failed bass expedition. On the north-western horizon, the islands disappeared into rain which had forgotten to be hesitant and had become a summer downpour.

What did they talk about, there on Rottumeroog as the winter nights closed in? What did they talk about, he in his English-flavoured Dutch ('..dat ik ben soe gelukkig…') salted with the forgotten elegance of French loan-words learned thirty years before at court? What music could the musicians play to drive away the frets of exile? How many candles would have to be lit, and prayers said? Or at the last, perhaps there was just merciless daybreak and a candle-end…

~

... 'Would *you* like to live on an island,' asked Monika, 'together with three mistresses?'

I said – it was a masterpiece of diplomatic evasion – that I'd prefer to live on an island together with a string quartet.

In some lights, Monika's hair is henna red. In others, it's chestnut brown. Seen against the sun, it's a filigree of blonde.

She is all my wives and mistresses.

She is all my islands.

38

9th August 2009
Avocets and spoonbills.

It's not merely ignorance which underlies my unfamiliarity with spoonbills. *The Complete Book of British Birds*, for instance (Cady and Hume, eds., 1988), doesn't list the spoonbill (*Platalea leucorodia*) as a species occurring within the British Isles, while Bruun and Singer's *Guide to the Birds of Britain and Europe* (1970, p.40) records that the bird occurs uncommonly. No wonder, then, that I never quite expected to see a spoonbill in this lifetime: the species occurs rarely if at all in those landscapes with which I used to be most familiar, and although I'd come across occasional references in Dutch guidebooks to spoonbills (*lepelaars* in Dutch), even those entries seemed to be muted in caution, and their short paragraphs sprinkled with words such as 'rare' and 'secretive'.

It was a surprise, then, when last week I saw not one spoonbill, nor two spoonbills, nor even three or four spoonbills. I saw a whole flock of them, a group of between forty and fifty birds.

I wasn't looking for spoonbills at the time. Together with my friend Marjoke Kuipers I was looking for avocets – that elegant wader which the Dutch so beautifully call a *kluut*, plural *kluten*. (The word *kluut*, modelled on the avocet's call, is deliberately onomatopoeic, rather like the word *curlew* in English.) I'd never seen an avocet, either, despite a half-hearted attempt a decade and more ago to spot these birds in England in the wetlands where they occur most abundantly, at Minsmere in Suffolk.

It was the Germans who were indirectly responsible for the reintroduction of the avocet to the wetlands of the British south and east coasts:

> *By the 1840s the avocet had become extinct in the UK, wiped out by marsh drainage, shooting and the taking of eggs by collectors. A century later, the coastal marshes of East Anglia were flooded to hinder the expected German invasion. This provided an ideal habitat for the avocet, which launched its own invasion. In 1947, four pairs were found on the Minsmere Level, which during the war had been a battle training ground. In the same year the RSPB agreed to lease the area and the reserve was born. In the years that followed The Scrape – a saline lagoon with shingle islands – was built and became home to a colony of avocets. Today the reserve is home to 100 of the country's 1,000 breeding pairs...*

http://www.wildlifeextra.com/go/news/minsmere-anniversary.html#cr – Accessed 9 August, 2009.

I like to think that the breeding pairs which quested through the Minsmere dyke in 1947 were birds which had come from this part of the world, from the Wadden. Here, the avocet is both relatively common and well established. A local wetland, tellingly named the *klutenplas*, is home to many breeding pairs in the summer, and it was to the *klutenplas* that we walked last week.

It was a hot and dusty afternoon, part of a sequence of hot and dusty afternoons which had kept the farmers busy with the harvest. Each morning one would see solitary figures standing in the middle of cornfields – men measuring the moisture content of the barley. By midday, the air would be full of dust as the combines went to work. Everything which could be set to combine a field of barley would be so set. Throughout the long afternoons, trailers would be pulled alongside the combines, and the grain offloaded. By teatime, the local roads would be sprinkled liberally with a dusting of corn from where the funnels on the trailers had leaked cereal. Occasionally, as light fell, one would see a farmer out there on the road-edge with a bucket and shovel, sweeping up the last grains: depending on one's point of view, this was either the public-spirited prevention of traffic accidents or parsimony run to harvest riot. (Thinking back to the farmers I've known, I preferred the parsimony.) All the while, until night smothered the travelling tractor headlight, the combining went on. I'm always reminded, during the grain harvest, of the time thirty-five years ago when I worked on a farm outside Hull, and how proud I was to have learned to reverse the tractor and grain trailer neatly – to the inch – under the chute which would transpose the grain from the trailer into the silo. Three tons of grain … and sweet, expensive corn dust everywhere.

On that afternoon by the *klutenplas* it wasn't the corn that was on our minds. It was the entire absence of avocets. A scan with the binoculars over the flat mud-rim of water which was brown with summer and algae revealed only occasional redshanks, the omnipresent and handsome oystercatchers and the usual, abundant flocks of duck, some wigeon and tufted ducks among them. I panned the far sky and the long, green horizon for a glimpse of black and white and that upcurved bill so wonderfully designed as a sieve. The only avocet I saw was painted onto a informative poster, set there by the local council, which announced that the *klutenplas* was well frequented with *kluten*.

Giving up on avocets, we climbed onto the top of the dyke nearest the sea. To the north lay Rottumeroog; to the north-east, the lighthouse on Borkum was clearly visible. But there, five hundred yards away, sitting as if stitched to the outermost rim of the land, was a row of white blobs which my eye and understanding at first dismissed as swans. Every twenty minutes, however, one of these birds would hoist itself into the air. The ungainly flight, the posture of the bird: trailing legs, outstretched neck … These were no swans. A friend of Marjoke's, who had appeared on his bike apparently from nowhere, uttered '…lepelaars'. Spoonbills. And so it was: what we were looking at was a relatively large flock of these birds – adult birds together with their fledged young – summering on the Wadden before making the long flight back to their winter quarters in Africa.

It never fails to surprise me, just how exotic these apparently muddy, unpromising coasts of the Wadden actually are. In winter, they're home to many thousands of geese, where the avian traffic runs from the Wadden northwards; in summer, they're home to visitors from Africa, and at that time the avian traffic runs southwards. All that traffic fetches up here, among the *kwelders* and their flat fish and crustaceans. Seen in that way, the Wadden is less a sea than an avian hub, the Chicago or Minneapolis of the European bird world. It is most remarkably abundant.

We walked back down to the *klutenplas* and the continuing absence of avocets. As we were finally turning homeward, back to the dust and combine harvesters, a spoonbill flew overhead, circled once over the water and came in to land. Even with the motor-drive whirring it was difficult to take more than one shot of the moving bird, and as it happened, the shutter picked up just one moment of flight. Yet that moment was enough for me to see the distinctive shape of the spoonbill, cruciformed and with those trailing legs which would soon and once again touch the red earth of Africa.

39

October 2nd, 2009
Owl holes: A theory of Dutch farmhouses

Nearly two months have passed, and I've failed to keep up this unreliable chronicle. Travel has intervened: endless railway journeys to and from Schiphol; time spent in the architecture of the 18th century in Bandon, Co. Cork; time spent in the 21st century in the isolation of cyberspace; time out of time spent looking at light move across a Kerry dawn breaking over Lough Currane. Meanwhile, summer has turned into autumn and the first of the falling leaves. The roads of het Hogeland are gobbed with mud thrown from tractor tyres and the autumn ploughing. A new academic year has begun amid chaos, overcrowded lecture halls and overfull and therefore dysfunctional email systems. Among vast tracts of time, there has been no time.

Where there was no time, I gathered into different crowds and was alone – Auden's phrase, which sums up a lifelong habit. There is no lonelier place than the periphery of the crowd which hapazardly contains the person who imagines they have no place. As I travelled, there was no one to talk to and I was often appallingly lonely. When I came back to what is not-quite-home, I was lonelier in many (though not all) ways than when I left. Meanwhile, some political voices insist that foreigners – specifically, some kinds of foreigners – are no longer welcome in the Netherlands. (The same kind of unwelcoming voices are often heard, in the same context, in the UK.) Occasionally I have been instructed by neighbours about the evils of foreigners. I suppose my neighbours intend to invoke Moroccans, Turks, Arabs-in-general – what is often perceived to be the threat of Islam – because somewhere in the conversation I will remind them that I am also a foreigner. Then comes the barely apologetic 'I don't mean you'. 'Unfortunately,' I invariably reply, 'you mean exactly and precisely me.' I try to explain that because I'm notionally white, was notionally reared as a Christian and notionally speak a bit of bad Dutch, then that doesn't exempt me from the 'foreigner' label.

I've looked for occasional consolations – in art, in the countryside, in land- and water-scapes. Equally occasionally, I've even found them. Three days ago, for example, as I was driving to and from Friesland, I found a strange kind of solace in thinking about the architecture of Dutch farmhouses.

Any visitor to the Netherlands who spends any time outside the large cities of the west will have seen a variety of Dutch farmhouses – styles of architecture which were exported both to England and to America, where they surface as what are known as 'Dutch barns'. Dutch barns have wide, oversized roofs whose inner space is capacious enough to hold a whole corn harvest. Similarly oversized roofs are found over many of the farmhouses in Friesland, where barn and living quarters co-exist in the same structure. The steep fall of these pyramid-shaped roofs is itself of interest, since it's designed to repel the maximum amount of rain maximally quickly. If, for example, one sat in a city office to design a structure which might hold a harvest, one would probably design something like a silo. If one garnered the harvest out there in the Friesland wind and rains, and imagined a geometry which might plausibly and efficiently contain it, the result would be a pyramid.

It must have been impractical, sometimes, sharing the same space with tons of husks. I imagine many dreadful winter mornings of dry-throated, allergic coughing. As prosperity grew into sociability, there would also be the matter of accommodating visitors. The result was the evolution of what the Michelin guide to the Netherlands (1999) calls the 'head-neck-trunk' (*kop-hals-romp*) farmhouse. In such a design, the living quarters (head) are separated from the barn (rump) by a short hallway (neck). Such farmhouses are found very typically in both Friesland and in this part of Groningen. Indeed, I live in a similar shape myself, although our *romp* contains additional living and working space rather than corn or potato sacks. Elsewhere, however, increasing agricultural prosperity in the 17th-19th centuries resulted in the evolution of the T-shaped farmhouse, whose original living quarters at the front of the barn were extended laterally, so that the final result comprises living quarters which form a transept to the barn behind them. The gabled, transept farmhouses, often constructed on three floors, are usually found in what were historically the richest areas of the Netherlands – in north and south Holland, close to the courses of the great rivers such as the Lek and the Waal.

I stopped the car on the way back from Friesland and considered a head-neck-trunk farmhouse that lay three hundred yards away across a recently ploughed field. There was wind and rain, and the ferrous smell of freshly turned autumn earth. The *romp* of the house – the barn – was tiled, not thatched, but retained small swan-decorated gables at either end of the ridge of the roof. In each extremity of the ridge, there in the 'V' formed by the roof timbers, was a hole.

I was mightily puzzled by those holes for several minutes. Why would a Friesland farmer wish to keep holes in his roof? But of course, if one thought about it – and I did think about it, held there in the raw irons of a cold, late September day – then the hole would supply much-needed fresh air to whatever perishables were stored in the barn. The holes, therefore, I reasoned, would be kept there to ventilate the stored crop.

I was quite wrong. These holes aren't air-holes. They're owl-holes – sufficiently large to admit owls, yet small enough to preclude the entry of larger predators. And why admit owls?

Mice. The Friesland farmers were deterring mice.

I've never been able to look at a Dutch farmhouse nor a barn since that moment without looking for the owl-holes – a solution to infestation and the practicalities of harvest storage which is as simple as it is elegant and ingenious.

And there (I thought to myself, in a rained-on Friesland) was a neat summation of the contradictions which seem to be inherent in those who think of themselves as 'native' to the Netherlands: clannish and often unsmiling – but also energetic and patient enough to be able to garden a country from an unpromising fen, and imaginative enough to be hospitable to predatory birds under the ridge of a barn roof. On the one hand, a group of people who are intolerant of Muslim head-scarves; on the other, a set who are creative with owls.

40

October 5th, 2009
The pike road

A nd there I was, travelling west again on the pike road.
We were in the middle of a two-day gale which blew from the north-west. The plum tree's late and dismal foliage was thrashing about. The air seethed. As I pulled the car onto the main road that links our village to the villages running west to Friesland, the roadside willows showed the whitened undersides of their remaining leaves. I was reminded, very briefly, of a poem I'd written many years ago, whose tagline was 'Willow, white willow'. I wrote that poem on the M6 motorway, driving north to Scotland from Lancashire while escaping a marriage that had sadly, unexpectedly, impossibly collapsed.

And there I was, travelling west again on the pike road.

October. Ploughing. Tractors. Mud on the roads. The clouds building on the northerly horizon until the horizon itself merges with cloud and becomes the one mass of driven rain. Past Baflo – the alleged home of those intricately dour

169

Christians who inhabit this part of what many local friends and neighbours refer to as the Dutch equivalent of the Bible Belt. Then a right turn: speed bumps slowing progress into the shortcut which leads out over the polder and in the direction of the Lauwersmeer.

And there I was, travelling west again on the pike road.
'The problem with the Netherlands,' my brother-in-law Peter had said to me, 'is that the horizon is always the same shape.' Perhaps it's a question of conformity with the sky that makes the Dutch themselves so often conformist. Behind the facade of liberalism lie the fussy ante-rooms which lead only to the terrible cultures of the demagogue. Outside there's only the permanent, unchanging oblong of the sky, whose autumn rainstorms hiss onto car windscreens.

Somewhere on the road to Lauwersoog, an autumn rainstorm hissed on the car windscreen. *And there I was, travelling west again on the pike road.*

Over the dyke which separates the Lauwersmeer from the Wadden. Giant sluices. The machinery which excavated a country from a mass of fen. The lake to the left a boiling mass of storm-stricken corrugations. Sunday traffic conforming neatly to the 70kph. speed limit. A snack bar surrounded by parked cars. The Dutch love affair with waffles, coffee, hotdogs and fat.

And there I was, travelling west again on the pike road, looking through diamonds on the windscreen for rumours of ospreys, birds which sojourn briefly over the grey clay and perch-haunted waters of the Lauwersmeer en route to Africa from Scotland. But the landscape and the waterscape are alike made out of rain: there are no ospreys. The reed beds at the western shore of the Lauwersmeer give on to a sullen mass of westward-running dead plumes, plant-spindles sick with rain-light. And then the solid ground of Friesland begins.

And there I was, travelling west again on the pike road.

The Dokkum by-pass.

There's nothing to say about the Dokkum by-pass except that it's on the Dokkum by-pass that the pike country really begins. The land is here still made predominantly from clay, but here and there lies a geological spur of peat or sand, and the canals lying on peat or sand run clearer than the clay-milk waters lying to the east. Clay and zander; clarity and pike. Clear water admits sunlight and therefore harbours more plants; plants provide cover, both for prey-fish and predators. Here, under the same October rains, is the country of the dabchick and the hunting grebe. Here is the starwort, here the dying beds of starving lilies whose wrack rots back into beds of what look like underwater cabbages. Stickleback and kingfisher...

And there I was, travelling west again on the pike road.

South-west now, past the turn-off to the Eeltjesmeer. The road signs are in two languages, Dutch and Fries. Fries, I remind myself, is the closest living linguistic relative of English, with which it shares the legacy of ancient sound-changes. In both languages, proto-Germanic <k> becomes 'ch' – *kirike* (an early loan-word) becomes 'church' in English while in Fries, the

171

same sound-change seems to take place only in front of front vowels – *tsjerk* not *tsjertsj* – but it's a semi-permanent reminder of how the linguistic past interferes nicely with the present. There are other similarities between the two languages. I pass a street sign which enjoins me to slow down and to watch out for 'us bearnen'. *Us bairns*. Our children.

And there I was, travelling west again on the pike road.

Finally, a left turn, and another left which takes me away from Aldtsjerk – 'Oldchurch' – and into the polder. The car is buffeted by squalls. I pull in to a parking space by a bridge whose footpath appears to lead to nowhere. On the back seat, the dog stands up expectantly.

Over the past three weeks I've tried to resuscitate a Hardy Fibalite spinning-rod which was made in 1974. I bought it second- or third-hand at a recent Dutch pike convention, and subsequently buffed it with car wax, applied oil and ferrule grease and revarnished its whippings. It's thirty-five years old and as good as the day it was made. Eight feet long, with a through action, it's ideal for fishing smaller and larger spinners in Dutch polder waters – long enough to keep the line clear of near-bank obstructions, flexible enough to fish varying weights and designs of spinner, tough enough to withstand the thousand natural shocks that rods are heir to and light enough to fish with one-handed all day. Above all, I'm comforted by the 'Made in England' logo etched so carefully into the metal of the reel-seat.

It's a dreadful cliché that human beings become more conservative as they get older. Unfortunately the cliché is also dreadfully true. I notice an increasing tendency to harrumph and to repine, and even to read the *Daily Telegraph* (a reading habit I wish could be removed by surgery), but underlying the tendency is merely wistful nostalgia and an awareness of how fragile and vulnerable all life, including human life, is. Baffled and hurt by the present, perhaps we simply retreat into the ideas of yesterday – anachronistic language, the manners of childhood, the habits of torn-off time.

I tackled up the Hardy while remembering Hardy's paper catalogues from the 1970s... Old pictures of someone spinning for salmon in the streams of the English north-east... The crest of the Prince of Wales adorning the advertising copy... "By Appointment" to the decades of sepia and sunlight... Fishing tackle that was quirky but reliable, almost invariably well made – and above all else, English.

I doubt the Hardy rod-builders of 1974 ever expected their rods to fetch up on the banks of a Friesland polder thirty-five years later. The destiny of these rods was supposed to be altogether more august – salmon, not pike; the well-heeled, not those who have had to fret about the price of a tank of unleaded.

And here I am, having travelled west again on the pike road.

Tess jumps from the car and goes off to inspect the verge-smells and to pee. I cast a tandem spinner in the direction of the far bank, allow the lure to sink – and immediately pull a surprised and surprising perch from the tea-coloured, gale-driven water. It's an early October Sunday. The earth stinks of iron, of decay, of blood in autumn. Rain reaches inside the lenses of my glasses. I'm exiled, middle-aged, worn out by work and by wrong choices. I return the bristling and indignant perch to the storm.

Why don't you go back to England? What are you doing in Friesland?

This is the pike road, and I'm at the end of it.

41

October 13th, 2009
Of spiders

Even the natural history field guides seem to be reticent about spiders. Dragonflies, butterflies, sedges, moths, beetles, even the various types of ant – they're all there in illustrated profusion. Yet of spiders there is typically scant mention, even though the order of spiders is vast: it comprises 40,000 species. True enough, north-west Europe is host to a mere fraction of these species, but even this fraction yields more abundance than the guides perhaps suggest. It seems a pity, too, that several guides seem reluctant to detail the predatory habits of spiders, which (even among the less spectacular northern European species) can be brilliantly designed. Even here, among the commonplace, predation can be so economical and well designed that its teleologies seem utterly beautiful.

The later summer and early part of the autumn seem to be a splendid time to watch spiders – or perhaps during this period the spiders are so busy with their prey that all their hunting strategies, including their webs, seem most apparent. Webs adorn the garden paths; the tops of hedges are hung with filaments; a trip to the outside woodshed for a basket of fuel ends with webs being wiped from the face. After a night of early frost, the dawn seems hung with lovely rigging where the low sun snags on ice-light.

For any angler, and particularly any fly-fisher, the chief value of spiders lies in their webs, which are diagnostic of what may (or may not) have hatched on, in and around the water the day or night before. Even a casual look in a spider's web, held there in the bushes, in the angle formed by the prow or stern of a boat, in the corner rafters of a fishing hut, will often reveal the water-borne prey of the previous 24 hours: hawthorns and smuts; duns and spinners; midges; greenfly, sedges and stoneflies. And there, somewhere – a giant in its own predatory world – will be the predator, running away from the disturbance up the guy ropes of its own construction.

I've peered myopically into spiders' webs for decades. It was only last week that I began to ask myself how a spider actually made its web. 'Some form of secretion,' I murmured to myself. But that wouldn't do. What sort of secretion? Secreted from where? How? Why, come to that, were spiders' webs at their largest and most overt during the autumn?

The last question was the easiest to answer. By the time August has turned into the sere and yellow leaf, the spiders born earlier that year have matured and are hunting. Moreover, their hunting is at its peak during this time of relative abundance of prey. Flies still hover; late wasps still core the remaining fruit; on and around the water there are sedges in profusion, and the autumn progeny of those flies which hatched the previous spring. In what, to different spiders, is a mixed hunting environment, ie. an environment in which more than one type of prey can be expected, it's common to find webs set at different angles, some lying horizontally (to trap insects rising from the water surface or returning to it to lay their eggs) or vertically (to catch airborne insects). On the other hand, webs lying horizontally are more likely to be destroyed by rain, so webs set at varying, more or less vertical angles seem to predominate, particularly among the commonest spiders likely to be encountered in this part of north-west Europe. These seem to be orbweb spiders, including *Argiope bruennichi* with its wasp-striped abdomen (dully and literally translated as 'wespspin' in Dutch), the Garden spider (*Araneus diadematus*, with a cross-mark – a diadem – on its abdomen) and *Zygiella x-notata*, which makes webs with a segment missing (see below) and which seems particularly common in and around our woodshed.

Back to 'some form of secretion'. The web-making procedure involves the conversion of proteins into silk. The process takes place via silk-emitting glands – 'spinnerets' – sited on the abdomen. As the silk is secreted, the spider uses its legs, which are attached to the thorax to draw the silk into place. A spider's silk is initially liquid, but – like epoxy, like certain kinds of fishing glue – it hardens when exposed to the air after it's drawn out of the spider's abdomen. This hardened, spider-silk is similar in tensile strength to nylon.

I imagined a spider's web made of the kind of nylon monofilament I use for fishing. It wouldn't work very well as a web, largely because the filament is smooth. If it were stretched tight into a web, any prey would also have the inclination to rebound from it, rather than being caught and held in it. A spider's web, therefore, and the silk from which it's made, must have the properties of being both sticky and relatively elastic. Both the stickiness and the elasticity are determined by the internal structure of the secreted silk. In making its web, therefore, a spider instinctively has to negotiate through a set

176

of predatory variables:

– if the web's too thin it won't hold larger prey; if too thick it's more visible to potential prey and therefore easier for that prey to avoid

– a horizontally set web is back-lit from the sky during daytime, and is therefore less visible to prey; but a horizontally set web is particularly vulnerable to rainstorms and falling debris

– a larger, verticallyset web is vulnerable to wind, particularly if it's constructed in an unsheltered place; a smaller, vertically set web is less vulnerable to wind but is also less efficient

– if the meshes of the web are set far apart then the web has a greater surface area and is therefore more likely to catch prey, yet a wide-spaced mesh may allow smaller prey to escape

– if the silk is too smooth and brittle, and the meshes set too close, prey may not be held efficiently in those meshes, ie. the web may not be maximally retentive

– if the hub of the web is set below the centre of the rest of the web then it will take the spider longer to reach its prey than if the hub is set above the centre of the web, since spiders find it easier to run downwards than upwards

Some spiders, including *Zygiella x-notata*, leave gaps in their webs. (Imagine an orange without a segment.) From my own observations it seems that one of the silk threads in or immediately adjacent to such a gap is slightly thicker, and that the spider uses this thread as a means of retreat to whichever corner of the web offers the most shelter. Furthermore, the hub of the web is likely to be set closest to this shelter point, so that the spider can reach caught prey quickly while retaining an optimally useful and perceptible line of withdrawal in case it, too, is threatened by predators.

I walked out into October's wan sunlight and was among the spiders. Webs hung in the camellias and across the surfaces of what in two weeks' time will be used as a small outside shelter for tender annual plants; webs hung in the woodsheds and trailed back into the still-unclipped ivy; webs occupied sheltered angles at the top of drainpipes and under the house eaves. The spiders scuttled in the beautiful intricacy of their rigging and retreated into their watchful, predatory hammocks, even as I stowed our own hammock on two hooks in the shed for the winter.

Epilogue

Almost like saying goodbye

I: Fishing and writing

In most years, early October still brings with it weather during which it's occasionally warm enough to enjoy coffee outside on a terrace. Eventually, however, it's again the falling leaf, the air's full of iron, rot, rain and ploughing and the terrace sun-umbrellas are furled at last. The first autumn storms shake the boughs of trees and the wind's full of leaf-litter. Mushrooms make a sudden appearance in year-mottled flower beds and in lawns gone dank; I imagine them nudging through the sward in the just-before-dawn darkness with a self-effacing shrug. As each days wears, headlights sluice past on the roads. In Usquert, as in villages reaching from the north-eastern Wadden through the Westerkwartier to Leeuwarden, a late October afternoon brings with it the smell of woodsmoke as fires and stoves draw into life.

The year's come full cycle. When I began writing these pieces, it was October 2008, the sea-trout season was almost over and the pike season had just begun. This year I began pike fishing towards the end of September, on the pike roads to Friesland, and over the past month, while the clocks changed and the year suddenly became tired, I've enjoyed a good month on, around and near the water.

Yesterday, for example, I was out in the float-tube on a small stillwater in Friesland – it's no more than a glorified pit from which turf and sand used to be extracted – trying to catch pike with the fly-rods. The pit was so steep-sided that it had only a minimal area of bankside shallows, and therefore weed couldn't easily root itself. Some small beds of pondweed clung on in corners of the lake, but in general the pike were to be found not in the weed beds but on the underwater shelf where two feet of water dropped to twelve feet and more. I spent most of the day working the tube and the streamer across the 2m-5m contour, which was clearly visible on a small fish finder I'd taken with me. While I was preoccupied with the pike and with the structure of the lake, the air began to turn purple and at last, a huge rainstorm dropped onto Friesland: the lake surface hissed with water drops and a guarded look up from under a wading-jacket hood revealed nothing except headlights half a mile away, coursing through the rain on the motorway. Meanwhile, I could feel the cold of lake water, which was leaking rather too readily through 5mm of neoprene into my right boot.

It's at those times that I ask myself most persistently 'Why do I do it?' Beyond the local, obvious and immediate answer ('Because in a strange sort of way I enjoy it') there's the question of what any angler is doing with his or her fishing rod. Here at the end of autumn, and at the end of another book, that question has also acquired a contextual relevance: I've spent a great deal of time in these pages, for instance, talking about fishing, and perhaps it would be wise to put that activity into a fresh perspective, merely as part of the way one can say goodbye.

I often think back to the image of the boy who was me: five years old, and instead of a fishing rod I have a crabbing net in my hands. With this net I rummage about under stones in the beck which ran through the fields at the back of Old Tan House in Bingley. A turn of the net-head, and the meshes hold caddis, snails and wriggling larvae (later I'd call them 'nymphs'). A minnow-hunt might last for many hours. Occasionally, too, a carefully turned stone would reveal bull-heads or stone loach. In spring, in standing pools in the cow pasture through which the beck ran, there would be tadpoles.

In any life there are what are now called defining moments. Generally, we're unaware of either the moment of definition or of what, of all the possible definitions, clusters on the moment. Vanishingly rarely, I have sensed such moments, but in 1963, at five years old, I was, of course, both inarticulate and heedless. Yet the moments of definition happened anyway, there in the crabbing net, and they took me to all the places in which I could intrigue with solitude and try to understand the intricacy of the life – the sheer, abundant, complex life – that lay in, on and around water. From those moments on, it became instinctive that I should try to have some sort of conversation with all that lay 'outside'. I had started to acquire the habit of talking to rivers, and as time flowed into the future what had been a crabbing net became a fishing rod and then a collection of fishing rods. In a simple sense, as the dialogues continue, our fishing rods are merely grown-up equivalents of jam jars and crabbing nets. They become tools with which we *acquire*, however briefly, in order to understand; they're vital parts of our diagnosis.

If the activity of rod-and-line angling is diagnostic then it doesn't surprise me that so many writers have themselves been fishers or have been attracted to angling. It's an astonishingly long list, running from ancient Rome through to Virgina Woolf and Ted Hughes. Yet writing, and in particular the writing of prose, has much in common with the activities included within angling. You'll recall, for example, that in the *Preface* to this book I claimed that while the making of poetry was aesthetic, the making of prose was profoundly forensic: it requires the extensive articulation of thematic links. It is precisely this, I suspect, that prose-making has in common with angling: they are both matters of context, of connection and linkage. Anglers and writers alike – they are diagnosticians.

What is diagnosed, and so often wordlessly diagnosed, out there on the canal- or river-bank, outside on the wind-riven spaces of the Irish loughs, under the great inverted bowl of the sky on the Danish coasts or in the glacial and haunted river valleys of Greenland? And what are the elements which in turn go to make up the diagnosis?

First, there is a *biological and meteorological* interest. What lies outside can be both complex and lovely, and often the loveliness is indexed in the complexity. Writers have known this – they have even overwritten it – from the earliest times. The angler, wrote the anonymous author of the 15th century *Traetise of Fishing with an Angle*, is drawn to places 'of swete ayre'; he will enjoy 'the swete sauoure of the meede floures'; he hears 'the melodyous armony of fowles' – and so on (and on). It's all true. Yet what I suspect the *Treatise* author was doing was using an extended set of localised descriptions – air, meadow flowers, bird song – whose metaphor implies a *rhythm*. Outside, the year has a very distinct rhythm. The air smells very different in December than in June; the flies that hatch on the river in April are rather different from those that hatch in July; pike lie in different ambush-places in May than the ones they favour in January; a February-running salmon is a rather different fish than the grilse which makes its way to the north of Scotland in August; the grayling is spawning in spring while the pastures turn green, but it's fit and active in the falling leaf; an east wind is a Continental, stuffy and humid waft in August whereas it's a bitter Siberian blast in February...

All those whose lives are governed by 'outside' – gardeners and farmers as well as anglers – know this, and know it intimately. Yet in the Western world in the 21st century both the knowledge and the intimacy are being lost, and as they vanish they're in danger of being misunderstood and even ridiculed. As societies have turned increasingly urban, as the lights must always be kept on, the loud music always play, the computer bring with it the illusions of company, intellect or conversation... As these things happen, we lose the rhythms of the life that surrounds us and we lose the weather. 'The weather' is of crucial importance to anyone who spends time outside, and part of my own angling is often a matter of Meteorological Man: it begins with the weather forecasts, days or even weeks before the line is threaded through the rod-rings. Included in 'the weather' is also a historical sense of connection: I know, for instance, that if the wind has a touch of north in it then the Dutch pike will usually hunt less readily than if the wind sits in another quarter; I also know that an east wind is the least favourable wind for fishing many of the Yorkshire Dales rivers for trout or grayling because in those places the east wind brings with it a lack of humidity which is in turn detrimental to a hatch of fly. How do I know these things? It's purely a matter of time, observation and making the necessary connections: the construction of a local, even a personal angling history.

If we become wholly urban we become merely whatever human detritus can be momentarily and trivially reflected in the plate-glass of a shop window in a mall. If our main hobby is 'shopping' – as many Britons pathetically claim it is – then there are no seasons, there is no smell, no rhythm in

185

a shopping centre. Cold is never cold; rain never falls; winter is never dark; the barometer neither rises nor drops: there's no weather. There's only the continual, expensive gasp of the air-conditioning and the terrible compulsions, all of them true. Confronted, then, with the shopping centre and its entire absence of rhythm, season and of anything that could be called history, I prefer the rhythm and the creativity of angling and outside.

Second, there's a *physical* interest. The 15th century *Treatise* author emphasised this, too: angling causes 'the health of your body' (which, added the author, is closely aligned with the health of your soul). We don't think, these days, in terms of *mens sana in corpore sano*. It's true that there's a sad mania surrounding mere physicality – gyms, exercise bikes, jogging – but I suspect that *mens sana* eludes us. It probably eludes us precisely because what's today called (somewhat quaintly) 'wellness' seems obsessive: it's so often about slimming, attractiveness and sex. We want to 'feel good about ourselves' not because we care about ourselves but because we care about what other people think of the selves that inhabit us. Or possibly, we're simply frightened – of that tyre of human lard, for example, and its capacity for inducing a premature heart attack. In this obsessive context, 'wellness' is a form of sickness whose chief components seem to be anxiety and loneliness. Even while the gym subscription tones us, the word 'soul' embarrasses us; we've unlearned the arts of human reciprocity and therefore of laughter; we've forgotten how to be sane.

The physicality of angling is by a gym-obsessive's standards no physicality at all. I don't care – or at least, I care less than I once did – about how other people think of the selves that are me; I see no point in worrying about my own death because it will happen anyway; and I'm not interested in how I look. Nevertheless, in the course of any given week I walk many miles both with and without the fishing rods. If I added up the distances I've rowed while fishing I'd probably reach well into four figures in the seconds it takes to finish typing this sentence. I've paddled away in float-tubes and climbed mountains in order to fish in tarns whose rumours of trout turned out to be cruelly untrue. I've sweated down the lengths of Irish estuaries in neoprene body-waders in search of sea-trout and have lost a stone in weight in the process. In any day's fly-fishing on any Dales river I'll cover what are miles of water, navigating past woodland, teetering on rock ledges, wading on the glib, algal smoothness of summer stones in thin current. I've heard otters call in darkness and set boat-drifts under the mew of osprey. My forearms have turned a radical brown in the summer sun, my stubborn face white, doughy and drip-nosed over the February pike-swim. Many anglers have done the same; many have done far more.

Within the physicality of angling there's also something more precise – timing, coordination, the use of power and delicacy. Casting a big pike streamer on a 9- or 10-weight fly-rod, for example, requires balance and physical judgement. It's more about timing – the timing of the forward cast, in particular – and less about muscular power, though some power must also be judiciously applied in the forward stroke of the cast. Done at its best, with precision and even elegance, casting those streamers acquires a rhythm, and therefore a physical satisfaction, of its own. In much the same way, perhaps, as a golfer sees a well timed drive sail arrow-straight 250 yards onto the welcoming greensward of the fairway I sometimes watch the pike streamer shoot out and upwards in a shallow ascending curve until it's checked by the pull of the fly-line against the reel, the line straightens above the water and falls, and the streamer angles out to drop neatly at the end of leader and trace adjacent to a bed of dying pondweed improbably far away ... There's a purely physical satisfaction in that: the timing has been perfect, the energy effortlessly transmitted, the cast immaculate.

This intimate kind of physicality, however, may be rather different from the gym or even from the golf. It's not achieved to impress others, nor done to win cups and prizes. Nor is the perfect cast a matter of force and sheer distance. The perfect cast covers the fish perfectly – appropriately, quietly, viably – whether those fish are lying 5, 15 or 25 yards away. 'The perfect cast' is simply a physically induced tactic whose intention is for the angler to continue his or her reciprocity with water and with fish. Done at its best, fly-casting is about strategic as well as physical grace.

Third, there's a *technical* interest. I enjoy – increasingly, I enjoy – the technical aspects of angling. Knots, splices and crimps; the properties and breaking-strains of differently constructed kinds of line; the different actions of fishing rods; line-speeds and the formation of D-loops; the construction of leaders and hook-links ...

I suspect I enjoy these things all the more because when I was small it was a commonplace family observation that I wasn't 'good with my hands'. Truly, I was once dreadfully clumsy and uncoordinated. Yet angling, and all the technical manipulations it has required over the years, has been very good for me: it's forced me to concentrate; obliged me to tie good, well made knots; encouraged me to tie flies to the extent that I now have thirty fly-boxes of various sizes filled with everything from size 24 dry-flies to tandem pike streamers 12 inches long. (Thirty fly-boxes. I write that phrase with something approaching shame, since embedded within it are all the winter-evening energies of what has possibly been an almost mis-spent life. Hours under the lamps with a succession of fly-tying vices ... and I've loved every minute.) More recently I've also been absorbed by the technical demands of, for example, fishing big pike streamers on spinning rods; of presenting coloured dead-baits to winter pike in clay-stained water; of trailing lures and baits at depth from the boat... These demands insist that at last I become 'good with my hands' as well as technically astute enough to realise how, for example, the different actions of different kinds of fly rod will translate into the transmission of energy to the fly-line. The dexterity and the astuteness have needed much practice, of course, but this form of practice, put at the service of the diagnosis that is angling, is seldom time wasted and it's invariably better than shopping.

Fourth, there's a *historical and literary* interest.

It pleased me, when I first came to live in the Netherlands, that there was a qualitatively impressive 20th century literature on Dutch fishing with which to engage. This literature, penned by men such as Jan Schreiner and others, focused largely but by no means exclusively on pike, and I spent a year or two learning to read Dutch by poring over those texts together with books from the middle of the last century detailing how some of the Dutch polders were constructed.

The pity of Dutch angling literature, however, is quantitative: there's relatively little of it. Habituated, as a native English user, to the chronological depth and range of English-language angling writing, one looks in vain for Dutch angling texts from, for example, the 18th or 19th centuries. Either they were never written or they have been lost to time. Therefore, once I had exhausted what little Dutch literature was available to me, I turned back to English, and to familiar texts such as Cotton and Nobbes from the 17th and 18th centuries, and behind them, to the 15th century *Treatise of Fishing with an Angle*. That is, I engaged again with the dialogues and small internalised dramas which reading has, for me, always brought with it.

Those dialogues and small, internalised dramas are why

I've written in *Outside* that writing is 'egocentric and anti-democratic'. To the reader who also writes, then in the act of reading no-one is ever equal. The dialogues one has with one's fellow authors are not those of equals: I am in no sense 'equal' in an angling context, for instance, to a Sawyer, a Skues, a Grey or a Cotton; nor am I equal to a Shakespeare, a Dante or a Horace. Nevertheless, my experience of reading these precursors is that I strive, always, to correct them, even to rewrite them. I would not respond to them in this way if I felt I was their equal: their voices are so much stronger than my own that in this trial of structural and thematic will and wit I can do no more than attempt to appropriate, exact, adapt and, in the end, produce a corrected version of whatever it was their works once were. Thus it was, for example, that the book I abandoned in 1997, called *The Other Side of the Stream*, is most intensely a form of dialogue with Grey's great *Fly Fishing* (1899) – and behind Grey, with the anthropocentric and therefore unreliable engagement with 'nature' propagated by Wordsworth (who happened to be Grey's favourite poet) and Keats. Thus it was, to take another example, that the 'Torquatus' section of *Polder* (2009) appropriated Horace's real-life friend and correspondent as an imaginary friend and addressee. These co-optings and creative rewritings are not in any sense 'democratic': one needs to be at least moderately able as a writer even to imagine one can engage in such dialogues, and one is also certain that in some sense one will fail – fail to engage, fail to subdue, fail to create anything worthy of taking its place in dialogue with the long-dead, still-living voices.

I ask myself sometimes whether others share any of these preoccupations. At one time, when I was much younger, and partly as a result of a liberal, classical and hugely useful early schooling, I imagined that such preoccupations were universally shared. But they are not: relatively few anglers seem to be particularly interested in the natural world which surrounds them; many poets and writers appear to be relatively unaware of the history out of which they write even as it allows them to exist at all. Many of us, that is, have become increasingly synchronic creatures, driven by the spawning of money and the getting of mere results in a quest for whatever a broken world esteems as success. The angler looks, perhaps, to the list of 'Personal Bests', the writer to the prize, the award or the placement on Amazon's sales list. Yet 'results' don't really interest me: to continue the dialogues which most engage me – with the natural world and with other thinkers and writers – I don't need to get results, but I do need to find interesting ways of posing useful questions, precisely so that the dialogues can continue. This is why I say that writing is a drama: there can be no drama without present or implicit voices, without questions and without surprising answers. Comedy, for instance, often poses an interesting question: 'Does an individualised destiny ever allow us to be happy?' The surprising answer is 'Yes'. Tragedy poses an aligned question: 'Will any individualised destiny ever cause us to be content?' The surprising answer is 'No'.

Posing the questions, respecting the models of strong precursors (to the extent that one wishes for a creative engagement with those models), responding to example, finding a voice among voices: these habits help me to find a sense of community and continuity in which I can at last feel if not 'at home' then at least in place. Nevertheless, because these predispositions seem to be so little shared by others – by which I mean living others – then they're often somewhat isolated predispositions. My habits of fishing and writing seem to belong most properly in a world to which they've already begun to say goodbye. Yet it's perhaps here, after all, that I belong: I belong outside.

II: England and Usquert

It was a shock, coming to live in het Hogeland in 2007. English visitors occasionally remark that the landscape is 'bleak'; Dutch visitors – those from Amsterdam or even from nearby Groningen – sometimes drive up to Usquert on the road bordering the Boterdiep and, once arrived, comment that Usquert seems like 'the end of the world'.

Three miles north of us and the road runs out. Beyond the road there's only the *kwelder*, the immensity of the saltings, and then the inverted bowl of the horizon greyly merging with the grey sands of the Wadden Sea: curlew, goose and mud flat; the continual wind; at night, a burnt moon rising in all her ochres.

Although it's ever-changing, this land- and seascape, it's also uncompromising. It insists merely, finally and always on itself: it cannot be co-opted into humanised tales of rural comfort involving bosky groves, amorous pursuits or picnics. It's not a place to lounge in sunshine with an opened bottle of wine. Summer, breathtakingly beautiful, is nevertheless brief: it's a meteorological shock rather than an extended conceptual space in which one can be at ease. Nor is this an easy place in which to laugh: instead of laughter, eyes narrow against the wind and the mouth's a hard, tired line whose contour tells only of time passing and lives enduring. What laughter there is lies in ritualised comforts – the village choir, the circle of weathered faces at a birthday party – but the fact that such Dutch comforts involve ritual emphasises, perhaps, that they are small comforts indeed.

~

I was recently visited, in connection with this book, by a photographer. Harry drove out to Usquert from Groningen in order to take some shots which would accompany Dutch translations of some of the pieces here into print. He walked into the courtyard outside our house and was greeted by Tess, who was as usual carrying the neoprene socks which she gives as a canine present to all our guests. 'Charming,' said Harry. 'Absolutely charming.' He meant the dog, the welcome, the house itself.

'You found us, then,' I said, for something to say.

'It's like driving to the end of nowhere,' said Harry, like so many of our visitors.

We fell into conversation about our backgrounds. Harry had been born in Groningen and then had migrated 'to the west' – 'Bright lights, big city... You can guess the rest.'

I could. But Harry was in one sense typical. So many Groningers move to the west (to Amsterdam, Den Haag, Leiden) and then, later in life, come back. It's as if the province of Groningen provides the Netherlands with the human equivalent of its spawning gravels. Natives migrate – but they very often come back, almost invariably to the same village (sometimes even the same house) in which they were born and raised.

The pattern of internal migration interests me because it gives the lie to what seem to be commonplace Dutch ideas about the status of foreigners who happen to be living in the Netherlands. Foreigners, it's often said, must 'integrate'. Integration seems to be a matter of conforming to Dutch 'normen en waarden' – Dutch 'norms and values'. It also seems to involve learning the Dutch language. Once these processes are accomplished, the migrant is said to be 'ingeburgerd' – naturalised.

The question of integration, as this matter is debated in the Netherlands (and in the UK), rests on very questionable assumptions. For example, many Dutch people, together with their politicians, appear to believe that a total isomorphism can obtain between *nationhood*, *residence* and *identity*. 'Nationhood' may be defined as the accident of birth announced in your passport. 'Residence' may be defined as the country in which you happen to be living. 'Identity' may be defined as that cultural and linguistic grouping to which you believe you most profoundly belong. In the views of so many Dutch people (and their politicians), the consummation devoutly to be wished is that a total isomorphism obtains between these three categories of definition. The 'typical Dutch person', for example, would in this dangerously over-simplistic view be defined as follows:

Nationhood — Residence — Identity
Dutch — The Netherlands — Dutch

Unfortunately, any person's sense of identity is seldom isomorphic with that person's nationhood and residence. Like English people, Dutch people often refer to define their own identity in terms of provincial, dialectal or even family allegiances:

Nationhood — Residence — Identity
Dutch — The Netherlands — Gronings

I'd contend, in fact, that a total isomorphism between these three categories is rather *rare*. Perhaps, after all, we are *all* migrants, *all* exiles – which would have the corollary (as David Knowles has privately pointed out) that *none* of us are exiles. And while I can see some telling *practical* similarities between them, I can't see any *conceptual dissimilarity* between

Nationhood — Residence — Identity
Dutch — The Netherlands — Gronings

and the following:

Nationhood — Residence — Identity
Dutch — The Netherlands — Islamic

or indeed the following:

Nationhood — Residence — Identity
British — The Netherlands — Probably Yorkshire

'Yes,' says a neighbour, 'but those Turks, those Moroccans... They're Islamic. We're not racist, but... They're not like us. They're the ones who are foreigners. In terms of integration... They're the ones we mean. We don't mean *you*.'

Yes, you do.

~

One of the distinguishing features of Dutch history is the ability of this society to export its citizens to other parts of the globe. Imagine, for example, a Dutch engineer living in the US. Does he or she feel any less profoundly Gronings, Drents, Fries or Amsterdams by the mere fact of his or her temporary or permanent residence in another part of the world?

Nationhood — Residence — Identity
Dutch — United States — Gronings

'Yes,' you might object, 'but that Dutch engineer can at least speak English, unlike so many migrants to Holland, who can't even speak Dutch.'

My profession is the English language. I've been hanging about the English language for nearly 52 years. I teach it, write in it. I know its structural limits as well as I know my own skin. I know (and teach the structure and history of) many of its accents. I'm afraid that from such a professional perspective the Dutch, generally speaking, aren't nearly as good at the English language as they think they are. For instance, I don't think it would be easy for a Dutch native speaker to engage with the English sense of humour, or its ironies, or English history and culture, if they were to migrate for any long period to any region of the British Isles. The difficulties involved would at least partly be of a linguistic nature – for even the most apparently 'fluent' of Dutch native speakers using English. In other words, *Dutch native speakers who happen to be resident in the country of their birth often seem to demand from migrants to that country cultural (including linguistic) skills and commitment which they would be incapable of delivering themselves in an analogous migratory position*. It's not difficult, that is, to imagine a position in which a Dutch native speaker found themselves in a position such as the following:

Nationhood — Residence — Identity
Dutch — England — Gronings

– and was assailed by the sense of so much cultural difference, so many linguistic challenges and so much loneliness that he or she would feel exiled from their own identity. In short, and whether they had or had not chosen their sojourn in a particular country of residence (or had had that chosen for them), they would feel displaced.

The debate about 'integration' also suffers from another, and serious, limitation. In order to learn a second, third or other language – and particularly, to do so in adulthood – the learner must be *motivated* to learn it. The surest way of motivating others, in any field of endeavour, is to provide a *positive example* to them. The learner must *want* to integrate with any non-native culture and language. In order to do the wanting, the leaner must perceive that culture and language as in some sense 'prestige'. (Here I use 'prestige' in what is a sense familiar to anyone who has studied how languages change. Speakers of languages acquire linguistic features which they think of as 'prestige', and discard – or simply will not acquire – features not so perceived.)

A migrant looks to Dutch language and society for any model which might be 'prestige'. What is there to admire, in that language and society?

I looked for things to admire, things with which I could engage (I've listed some of them below). I wanted, I think, to 'fit in'. Like any migrant, I was looking for a model to which I could aspire. It would have been nice to think that I was motivated to 'integrate'.

I was told, explicitly, that I did not 'fit in'. Like many foreigners resident here, over the past ten years I've watched as successive politicians tell us in different ways that 'The Netherlands is full'. I've watched as Dutch politics, like so much British politics, has descended trivially into demagoguery and posturing. I've listened, carefully, to the voices of permanent

197

resentment on both sides of the debate about what constitutes 'integration'. I've heard the bafflement as so many Dutch people wonder aloud about a nation they no longer recognise. I only add here that many English people wonder the same about England. Where have we gone? What on earth are we becoming?

English people occasionally tell me that the Netherlands is 'liberal' and 'tolerant'. The only reply is a mirthless smile. 'Yes,' says another neighbour, 'but we – the Dutch – have freedom. You can write whatever you want. You can dissent.'

I can indeed write whatever I wish. I insist on that freedom, and insist on defending it if only because so many human souls have died to ensure I have this privilege. But just try 'dissenting'. Try proposing, for example, here in the Netherlands, that 'dé Nederlander bestaat niet' (Princess Maxima of the Netherlands, speech given in 2007) – that the 'typical Dutch person' doesn't exist. As it happens, Princess Maxima and her speech writers were quite correct: as I've claimed above, there's no natural or even necessary isomorphism between nationhood and identity. It was a hugely brave and intelligent thing to say. It met with a furore of protest.

And what to do, finally, about the following individual?

Nationhood — *Residence* — *Identity*
British — The Netherlands — Probably Yorkshire

Has such an individual nothing to contribute to the country in which he finds himself resident? Would that individual feel motivated to want to contribute anything whatsoever to a society and culture which has already told him – as they have told many other migrants – that he doesn't, that they don't, 'fit in'?

'If you don't like it here, then go home.'

I can't. Motivated by the usual suspects, love and money, such was my original commitment to living in the Netherlands, to learning Dutch and to attempting to contribute at least something to the society that surrounds me that, characteristically, I burned all my bridges. There's no road back, and even if there were, I'm not sure whether I any longer feel a sense of identity with the 'England' into which I was born. If I do feel any sense of identity it's with an England which is vanishing and perhaps has already vanished.

Last night I gave a talk which touched on some of the ideas explored here. The kind Dutch audience listened politely and patiently to whatever I had to say, and I was most grateful to them. And yet... One comment, during the questions which closed the evening, was that 'You chose it. You chose to come here, didn't you?'

I did so choose, and it was one of the most difficult decisions I've ever had to make. I am, yes, responsible for that choice. I blame no one else for the sense of dislocation and exile I sometimes feel. Yet the commentator might as well have said 'If you don't like it, then go home'. He also seemed to imply that 'exile' was too strong a word for the sense of disclocation I was exploring. Perhaps it is. But whether one has been dislocated by choice or by real or imagined wrongdoing the imaginative result is the same if one cannot go back. Further, during what was a long honeymoon with Dutch matter, back in 2000-2003 when I first came to live here, I rarely felt the way I do now: the structure and predispositions of Dutch society seem to have changed over the past ten years – become harder, more careless, less compromising and more resentful. The voices of insistence – again, voices on both sides of the debate about 'integration' – seem ever more strident.

There are still many things to admire in this, Dutch, society. Dutch management of natural resources, including that of water, is probably the best in the world. National planning – particularly the planning of the Second Delta Project, which will raise the sea dykes, take 100 years to complete and cost 100 billion Euro – can seem breathtakingly imaginative. The management of national parks, open spaces, lakes and seashores is often acutely sensitive. The train service – much of it still in national ownership – is both cleaner and much more reliable than that in the UK. Public facilities – toilets, libraries, parking spaces, roads – are generally good. The cultural history of the Netherlands is explored in many accessible galleries and museums. The health service is affordable and unusually kind and efficient. Dutch pike anglers are among the best – most farsighted, adventurous, most technically astute – on the planet. One also still hears, if only here and there, some wise, generous and openminded views: after the talk yesterday evening, for example, a Dutch gentleman seized me by the hand, shook it vigorously, and told me that '"Integration" is the most stupid word the Dutch ever invented.' He was smiling as he said it, too. I won't forget that.

If this has been exile, allow me to repeat it has been a beneficent exile. In very many ways, I've been bloody lucky. Perhaps, after all, the last word here should belong not to the Dutch and not even to me, but to my mother. Three months ago, over afternoon tea in England, she listened carefully and patiently to my middle-aged bafflement. When I'd done, there was a short pause. Logs crackled and shifted with a whoosh in a hotel grate; there was the clink of cutlery. 'Dear, dear Chris,' she said, 'you're just homesick.'

I am. But wherever home once was, it's there no longer. Perhaps this is why so many displaced persons and migrants cling onto their versions of religious certainties: they replace the inevitability of nostalgia with the illusions of permanence. I'm also beginning to suspect that the place that most of us consider most deeply to be 'home' is the place called childhood:

Nationhood — Residence — Identity
Irrelevant — Anywhere — Childhood

If one is lucky (and many are not), then there – in childhood – is the circle of schoolfriends, the shared assumptions with and within which one grows up, the sense of curiosity that will quickly and always replace the sense of resentment. It's there that one speaks the language that is not for nothing called a mother tongue. And yet, therefore, if childhood (more properly, the illusion of childhood) most narrowly constitutes our identity, *none of us* can go back. The past, merely by the fact of being past, has already estranged us.

Homesick, uncertain, unable to go back ... Where do I go? I must relearn simply to be grateful for what I've had, if not for whatever it was I did. Like the successful Irish exiles in London so touchingly evoked in Cathal O'Searcaigh's wonderful recent memoir, *Light on Distant Hills* (2009, p.227), I must relearn to commute again between past and present. That is almost certainly a rather less well travelled road, but perhaps it, too, leads beyond regret and into the future – and in doing so, is part of an outsider's journey home, defined here in adulthood as *that place in which one never feels one is always almost saying goodbye.*

III: Home and outside

'Home', that is, is Hello. It is smiling recognition. It's not the condition of more or less fixed resentment which I so often find around me and sometimes find within myself. Resentment, after all, is merely anger spread thinly across time, and because anger is anger it's always shaking there on the brink of some terminal goodbye.

Smiling recognition depends on the prior existence of unconditional acceptance, and (again, if one is lucky) the most reliable place in which to find that acceptance is in childhood. Stranded here on the island of today, of course I feel the pull of that imaginative, powerful and historical Hello. It's the pull of nostalgia.

'Nostalgia' is probably one of the most beautiful words the Greeks ever loaned to the English language – but one should beware of Greeks bearing such gifts. The condition of nostalgia, for instance, is an imaginative response to the difficulties and threats perceived to lie in the present. In that sense, nostalgia is a recreative form of *consolation*. Unfortunately, all forms of consolation are almost always false, as the philosopher Irish Murdoch claimed. That is, most commonly, consolation depends on self-generated images, and for all that we can never exist without them, such images are traps.

Two months ago I spent some time in Yorkshire. I was fishing, with a view to constructing two or three feature articles for *Trout and Salmon* about fly-fishing for grayling in the Dales rivers. On the first day I drove from Scarborough to Ripon, north past Masham and Middleham and from there to Richmond. I remembered childhood teas with aunts in Harrogate; stale tea in thermos flasks; hot tea with fish and chips; tea everywhere. On the second day I drove south again past Middleham, and remembered a school project I completed (just three fells away) as a ten-year-old about Richard III. On the third day I revisited the river Aire, the river which governed, one way or another, large parts of my childhood. On that third afternoon I stood in teeming rain and took photographs. When the light and the clouds lifted I strained my eyes for a glimpse of Eldwick Moor to the south-east, and for the edges of hills which led into the valley whose slopes held and still contain my first school. The contours of all the hills were entirely familiar. I could reconstruct the etymologies of all the place names; the accent of the West Yorkshire dialect still spoken in Skipton (another school project – Lady Anne Clifford and the English Civil War) was little changed from the accent which often surrounded me as I was growing up. Even the numbers on the buses which ran to Gargrave to Skipton and from Skipton and the Aire Gap down to Bradford didn't seem to have changed. The pubs and hotels were still in business and still had the same names. As the camera shutter clicked and I went about trying to catch a grayling I was at least partly smiling with recognition. It felt, in a way, like a kind of very minor homecoming. Yet the feeling was merely nostalgia – a trap.

If I recreate this childhood home now, in middle age, I must do so by selecting and therefore by falsifying. I select, that is, the most consoling and satisfying images: the young boy with the crabbing net, for instance; the schoolboy doing his prep. in a Latin primer and discovering the delight of translating from Latin into English and then back again. Those images are true enough – but they are not the whole truth, and I'm sure that the boy with the net and with the Latin primer wasn't quite as settled and happy as I now imagine him. Childhood for him, as for everyone, also had its puzzles, even its terrors. Nor was English society, back in the 1960s, altogether as safe, secure and polite as I now imagine it must have been. If I had to characterise it most truly I'd say it was a *more heedless* kind of society: the English, after all, had won a war, had only recently given back an Empire, and often, effortlessly assumed that they were culturally superior to everyone else. It comes as a shock, now, to realise that the portraits and images which hung most prominently in the school where I did that Latin prep. were those of the Queen, Winston Churchill, and the England cricket XI. I suppose that I was being trained to become at best some sort of unimportant functionary in a British Empire which no longer existed. There was fog in the English Channel and the Continent was cut off…

The assumptions, so many of the attitudes and even parts of the training and education seem risible now – as laughable as the notion of 'fair play'; as absurd as the word 'decency'; as indecent as the word 'gentleman'. Yet the past, all its contemporaneous illusions and mistakes, and all the illusions and errors which now sustain merely the *idea* of 'the past', were necessary to support what is simply the idea of Now. Images piled on images: I rootle through them, sort them and sift them like someone obsessively clearing the junk in an attic. They bring me only, as Yeats so terrifyingly promised, into 'the desolation of reality'.

What did Yeats mean by desolation? The word calls up further images: the bleak, the otherworldly, the end of the road, the scarred moorland browning in winter under the wet and bitter wind. Yet I doubt that's what Yeats meant, and suspect rather that he meant desolation to be defined as *that imaginative place in which there can exist no consolation*. It's the place where all of us must go when our revels now are ended. Autumn rain streaks down the fairground's wooden ponies and thrown anyhow into a corner lie the remnants of Prospero's broken staff.

~

Autumn's turning to winter. The garden blackens in its relics of summer. If I step from the house for a moment then the outside air carries the stain of wood ash from village fires. Every half-hour the church clock strikes. A neighbour is timbering a roof. Greenfinches are busy at the bird feeders hanging from the apple tree. I can hear the jackdaws in the churchyard grating on each other in a squall of complaints. So much rain has fallen over the past two weeks that the winter barley is glazed with rainwater and has become not a crop but a view which reflects only the underside of continual grey cloud.

And have there been no consolations?

There has been kindness, yet kindness isn't a consolation but an activity.

There has been the joy of describing the natural world, yet description isn't a consolation but a procedure.

There has been fishing, and within the fishing, friendship, yet both have been so extensive and intricate that they haven't existed in a recollective pause filled with nostalgia but in real time whose structure is rooted in water.

I step back inside the house. There's a waft of baking from the kitchen: Monika has been making German biscuits for Christmas. Tess hears me come in, brings me the neoprene socks.

I climb the stairs to the study. The windows look out onto roofs and weather-vanes. There's the smell of books, polish, varnish from last night's fly-tying session. A 10-inch-long pike streamer is pinned to a cork board to dry.

There has been love, too – abundant, generous love – yet to conceive that as a consolation would be to think one deserved it. I have not deserved it, and yet I have received it (and given it) anyway. Unearned, vastly surprising, the only way I can begin to discover words in which to describe it is to reach back into what seems to be an antique English vocabulary containing the lexical register of pity and miracle, mystery and blessing. These things were there in time long before Prospero's magic and will be there long after the magician's staff is dust. Magic may be stardust, but it's nevertheless only dust; pity and miracle, mystery and blessing are, like goodness, timeless.

Stranded on the island which constitutes all the moments of Now, disturbed by the impossibility of fitting in, nagged at by mere nostalgia, I suspect that, caught in the pettiness of resentment and the continual headache that is the getting of money, I have forgotten pity and miracle, mystery and blessing. They seem to exist outside anything, yet inside everything. And precisely because they belong both inside and outside ...

Finally, among fishing rods and books, this is where I can say Hello.

Inside that belonging, I also belong outside.

Acknowledgements

Some of these pieces, including 'The roach-fishers of Uithuizen', which provided a model for what was to follow, first appeared in *Waterlog*, and I'm most grateful to Jon and Rosie Ward-Allen for allowing me to use these pieces here. Valerio Cugia was kind enough to comment on some of these pieces, and suggested several improvements in structure and tone.

Marrie Kuipers translated some of the pieces which followed that initial impetus into Dutch, and I'm also particularly grateful to her, a native of het Hogeland, for helping me to understand many aspects of the cultures and peoples of my adopted home. Some of her translations have appeared in the Dutch journal *Noorderbreedte* in 2009-10, and in that context I'm most happy to acknowledge the help and support offered to me by Annemarie Kok, Agmar van Rijn and Harry Cock. On the appearance of the first of Marrie's translations (*Noorderbreedte #5*, December 2010), I was subsequently contacted by Jan Teuben, who kindly and helpfully corrected some errors of both detail and supposition relating to how natives of het Hogeland experienced World War II and its aftermath. I am most grateful to him.

Powell Ettinger, the editor of *Wildlife Extra*, kindly allowed me to to reproduce a short passage about the spoonbill which is here embedded in piece 38, ('Avocets and spoolbills').

Monika was there all along: not only did she read and comment most usefully on parts of the typescript, but also, as the text describes, she was and is all my islands.

References

Text

Anon. (1999) *Michelin Guide to the Netherlands*. Watford: Michelin Tyre plc

Belloc, Hilaire (1912) *The River of London*. London and Edinburgh: T.N. Foulis.

Brouwer, Tako, Ben Crombaghs, Ate Dijkstra, Albert Jan Scheper, Peter Paul Schollema (2008) *Vissenatlas Groningen Drenthe*. Bedum: Uitgeverij Profiel.

Bruun, Bertel (1970) *The Hamlyn Guide to the Birds of Britain and Europe*. [Illustrated by Arthur Singer.] London: Golden Pleasure Books.

Buchan, John. (ed., 1982) *Izaak Walton and Charles Cotton: The Compleat Angler*. [Oxford World's Classics edition, reprinted from the first edition, 1935.] Oxford: Oxford University Press.

Buller, Fred and Hugh Falkus (2001) *Dame Juliana: The Angling* Treatyse *and its Mysteries*. Moretonhampstead, Devon: The Flyfisher's Classic Library.

Cady, Michael and Rob Hume (eds., 1988) *The Complete Book of British Birds*. Basingstoke, UK: AA and RSPB Publications.

Chinery, Michael (ed., 1987) *Kingfisher Field Guide to the Wildlife of Britain and Europe*. London: Kingfisher Books.

Clarke, Brian and John Goddard (1979) *The Trout and the Fly: A New Approach*. London: Ernest Benn Ltd.

Courtney Williams, A. (1973) *A Dictionary of Trout Flies*. [First edition 1949.] 5th edition. London: A.&C. Black.

Edlin, Herbert L. (1975) *The Observer's Book of Trees*. London: Frederick Warne and Co. Ltd.

Fey, Toon (2002) *Wadden: Gids voor Liefhebbers* [Wadden: A Guide for Enthusiasts]. Abcoude: Uitgeverij Uniepers

Grey, Edward (Viscount Grey of Falloden, 1899) *Fly Fishing*. London: J.M. Dent and Co.

Grey, Edward (Viscount Grey of Falloden, 1927) *The Charm of Birds*. London: Hodder and Stoughton.

Hayward, Peter J. (2004) *Seashore*. London: Collins New Naturalist Series.

Hudson, W.H. (1902) *British Birds*. London: Longmans Green and Co.

Kingsmill Moore, T.C. (1979) *A Man May Fish*. [First edition 1960.] Gerards Cross: Colin Smythe.

Macan, T.T. and E.B. Worthington (1972) *Life in Lakes and Rivers*. Revised edition. London: Collins/Fontana.

Malone, E.J. (1998) *Irish Trout and Salmon Flies*. [Reprinted from the 1993 Flyfishers' Classic Library edition.] Machynlleth: Coch-y-Bonddu Books.

Muus, Bent. J. and Preben Dahlstrom (1971) *Collins Guide to the Freshwater Fishes of Britain and Europe*. [Edited by Alwyne Wheeler.] London: Collins.

O'Searcaigh, Cathal. (2009) *Light on Distant Hills: A Memoir*. London and New York: Simon and Schuster.

Postma, Reinder H. (2007) *Donough McCarthy: 4th Earl of Clancarty*. Oudwoude: Trion Kollum/Gemeente Kollumerland.

Raymo, Chet (2001) *An Intimate Look at the Night Sky*. London: Vintage.

Righyni, R.V. (1968) *Grayling*. London: Macdonald.

Stichmann-Marny, Ursula and Erich Kretschmar (eds., 2002) *ANWB Natuurgids*. [German text 1994/2000. Stuttgart: Franck-Kosmos Verlags-GmbH & Co.] Den Haag: ANWB Publications.

Swier, Ad (2006, edited by Chris McCully) Passion for Pike. Lichtenvoorde: Westerlaan.

Thomas, R.S. (ed., 1964) *Selected Poems of Edward Thomas*. London: Faber and Faber.

URL

Bass on Borkum (Germany): http://www.borkum.de/index.php?sid=1289)
Accessed July 30th 2009.

Spoonbills at Minsmere (UK): http://wildlifeextra.com/go/news/minsmere-anniversary.html#cr
Accessed 9 August, 2009.

Two Ravens Press is the most remote literary publisher in the UK, operating from a working croft by the sea, right at the end of the most westerly road on the Isle of Lewis in the Outer Hebrides. Our approach to publishing is as radical as our location: Two Ravens Press is run by two writers with a passion for language and for books that are non-formulaic and that take risks. We publish cutting-edge and innovative contemporary fiction, nonfiction and poetry.

Visit our website for comprehensive information on all of our books and authors – and for much more:

- browse all Two Ravens Press books (print books and e-books too) by category or by author, and purchase them online at an average 20% discount on retail price, post & packing-free (in the UK, and for a small fee overseas)

- there is a separate page for each book, including summaries, extracts and reviews, and one for each of our authors, including interviews, biographies and photographs

- you can also find us on Facebook: become a fan of the Two Ravens Press page, and automatically receive all our news and updates about new books.

www.tworavenspress.com